BOROUGH OF TWICKENH RY SOCIETY

PAPER NUMBER 27

HAMPTON IN THE NINETEENTH CENTURY

by

G. D. HEATH

October 1973
2nd Edition February 1993

Price £3 50

NOTE TO THE 1993 EDITION

This comprehensive yet succinct account of Hampton in the Nineteenth Century was written by Gerald Heath, to whom the Borough of Twickenham Local History Society and the residents of Hampton are greatly indebted, not only for his meticulous research into local history, but for the qualities of integrity, friendliness and humour which he brought to all he did, both in the development of the Local History Society (of which he was Chairman 1968–1971) and in charitable and community activities in his adopted home, Hampton. Gerald died at the age of 75 in June 1988, and friends have given donations towards the provision of an Archives room in Hampton Court Palace, to whose history he made a major contribution during the last fifteen years of his life. His extensive research, and the range of his interests, is well reflected in this booklet, which has been out of print for many years. When it was first published, the Local History Society Papers were only modestly illustrated, and for this new edition we have added eight additional pages of illustrations, selected by John Sheaf from his own collection and annotated by him. Joan Heath has provided the originals of the two drawings by Mrs D.E.Ablewhite, enabling us to reproduce them more clearly than in the original edition. The map has been completely redrawn by Anthony Beckles-Willson, to whom we are very grateful. No alterations have been made to the text, and the reference to the nursery land at the foot of page 45 remains as written. We are much indebted to the Hampton Fuel Allotment Charity for a grant which has enabled us to produce this reprint.

ISBN 0-903341-57-3

ILLUSTRATIONS

Figures 3, 11 and 13 are reproduced from photographs contained in the Subscribers' Edition of Henry Ripley's "History and Topography of Hampton on Thames", 1884. Page numbers indicate references in the text.

Fig. 11. **The Waterworks c. 1880;** these developed in Hampton as a result of an Act of 1852 which forbad taking water from the tidal Thames; Hampton was the first practical site above Teddington Lock where works could be established. The Grand Junction, Southwark and Vauxhall, and West Middlesex Companies had all built plants in Hampton by 1855.

Fig. 12. **Headquarters of a Regatta on Garrick's Lawn,** In front of Garrick's Villa and beside Garrick's Temple. There were a number of Regattas held between Hampton and Molesey, the most famous of which were the Hampton Watermen's Regatta, first held in 1835, and the Molesey Regatta. (p. 17)

Fig. 13. **Red Lion Square 1875.** This can be dated precisely, as this was the only year in which Lewis the Baker and Deeks the Grocer occupied adjacent shops, as shown. The Red Lion was destroyed by fire in 1908 (see Fig. 18), and the current building (now converted to offices) was built in 1909. (p. 3)

Fig. 14. **Thames Street looking east towards St Mary's Church and the Bell Hotel,** showing some of the numerous shops and businesses which flourished there before the age of the motor car. Note the signboard across the roadway for the Red Lion and Will Weech the landlord. (p. 3)

Fig. 15. **The Old Grammar School;** the foundation stone was laid in 1879, after it had occupied a number of other buildings. After the school's removal to its present site in Hanworth Road, the building was used for various purposes, including adult education, before it was demolished. (p. 26)

Fig. 16. **Hill House, used as a school c. 1837-1854.** The building was demolished in 1902 for the Station Road filter beds. This is believed to be one of the only two pictures of it in existence. (p. 31)

Fig. 17. **The Hampton Volunteer Fire Brigade established by Fire Brigade Captain Robert Graham,** who lived in the riverside house "St Albans", in 1885. He is the bearded figure in the centre. (p. 50)

Fig. 18. **The Fire Brigade in action at the fire which destroyed the old Red Lion in 1908.** The fire was started deliberately as practice for the Brigade, as it was due to be demolished to build a replacement. A movie film, which still survives, was made of this event. (p. 3)

HAMPTON IN THE NINETEENTH CENTURY

by G. D. Heath

The Saxon Manor of Hamntone, as described in the Domesday Book, and likewise the mediaeval parish of Hampton, comprised the Town of Hampton and the Hamlet of Hampton Wick. In between, straddling the Town and Hamlet, was Hampton Court. It was perhaps not surprising that the Hamlet, being some way distant, resented its dependence on the Town and the two were in dispute for more than two hundred years, even to the extent of taking legal proceedings one against the other on at least two occasions. The first stage in the separation of the two came in 1830 when the old parish church of St Mary was rebuilt and a new church was built at Hampton Wick serving the new ecclesiastical parish of St John. The rift widened further in 1863 when the parish of Hampton Wick decided to adopt the Local Government Act of 1858 and to form its own Local Board. The Town, on the other hand, persisted in the system of local government by Vestry.

With the rapid growth of the Town in the direction of Hampton Common the need for a new parish became evident and the parish of St James, New Hampton, was constituted in 1863. By popular demand the name of the new district was changed to Hampton Hill in 1890. Meanwhile the parish of St Mary continued to grow towards the north-west and the formation of a new parish was mooted as early as 1886, but it did not materialize until 1908 with the building of All Saints' Church. This paper is concerned only with the history of these two parishes which now constitute Hampton-upon-Thames.

HAMPTON IN 1800

No map showing Hampton in accurate detail appeared before 25 inch to the mile Ordnance Survey of 1864-70. Even the 1804-06 2 inch O.S. map is inaccurate in some respects. The sketch map at Fig. 9 has been constructed by taking as a frame-work the system of roads and lanes shown on maps before and after 1800, namely Rocque's map of 1754, Cary's map of 1786, the 2 inch O.S. map, the Enclosure Award maps (1811-1826) and the map in the Court Rolls relating to the sale of the Manor House estate in 1820. Further topographical details, such as field names, are based on property descriptions in the Court Rolls of the period. The map also shows the position of the private houses and inns referred to in the text.

The Census return of 1801 shows there to have been 1,722 inhabitants in Hampton Town consisting of 290 families living in 134 houses; 7 houses were unoccupied. Almost all the houses and lands were copyhold of the Manor of Hampton Court. From 1830 onwards many of the copyholders enfranchised their property and by 1900 nearly all of the larger houses and many of the smaller ones became freehold.

The sketch map shows the common land which was later enclosed under the Hampton Enclosure Act of 1811. Many of the smaller plots allocated by the Enclosure Commissioners were sold or exchanged shortly afterwards, Mr James Campbell of Hampton Court House acquiring 39 of them to add to the farm he then owned known as Chalk Farm, later known as Tangley Park Farm.

HOUSES, PUBLIC AND PRIVATE

The Register of Alehouse Keepers for 1800 lists ten public houses in Hampton, the Maidenhead, Black Horse, Red Lion, Lamb, Jolly Coopers, White Horse, World's End, Bell, Crown, and White Hart. Hampton's most celebrated inn, The Feathers, which had been parish property since the 16th Century, had ceased to be an inn about 1790 and so is not included. Another of Hampton's inns, the Old Tavern, which stood at what is now the southern end of Plevna Road, also ceased to be an inn about 1780.

Six of the inns of 1800 exist to this day – the Jolly Coopers; the Maidenhead, renamed the Duke's Head about 1874; the White Hart, named the Six Bells until purchased by David Garrick about 1773, was rebuilt in 1901; the Bell, rebuilt after the disastrous fire of 1892; the Red Lion after its demolition by fire in 1908; and the World's End in 1901. Of the remainder, the White Horse, formerly the Londonderry Arms, ceased to be used as a public house in 1914 and is now the private house "Compton" in High Street. The Black Horse stood where Nos. 51 – 61 Station Road now stand until the licence was given up in 1854. The Crown's licence was given up in 1909 and it is now the private house No. 38 Thames Street. The Lamb ceased to be an inn about 1800; it stood in Thames Street, somewhere near to the house known as The Box.

In the eighteenth century Hampton had achieved a high reputation as a residential area. Indeed W. P. Phillimore, in a preface to his transcription of the Hampton marriage registers, wrote, "as fashionable resorts Hampton and Twickenham were probably unrivalled in the United Kingdom in the eighteenth century". At that time the seaside had not started to exercise its powerful influence on the leisured classes, but the River Thames, despite its insalubrious qualities, proved a strong attraction. David Garrick is reported to have said "I must have a river" and he spent the days of his prosperity in houses overlooking the Thames at Hampton and in London at the Adelphi. Twickenham and Hampton also had the advantage of being at a convenient distance from London by carriage. There is little reason to suppose that Hampton owed its popularity to its location near Hampton Court Palace. Indeed it was not until the Palace had lost its popularity with the Sovereign that Hampton attained distinction as a resort.

In the first half of the eighteenth century Hampton's wealthier residents were mainly London merchants with a sprinkling of the lesser nobility. The Fredericks at the Manor House and the Primatts at Hampton House (later Garrick's Villa) were grocers and spice importers. Charles Jervas, the King's Sergeant Painter, was an occasional resident at Elm Lodge (otherwise The Elms) from 1734 to 1748, and Edward Lovibond, a minor poet, lived there from 1748 to 1775. It cannot be doubted that Hampton received a fillip when David Garrick decided to buy Lacey Primatt's house in 1754. After David Garrick came John Beard, the great Handelian singer and patentee of Covent Garden, who lived at the house later known as Rose Hill, now the Hampton Public Library. Thomas Rosoman, the founder of Sadlers Wells, lived at Jessamine House (Fig 8) from 1772 till his death in 1782 and the house belonged to his descendants until ca. 1870.

The Countess of Pembroke, with whom Garrick was on friendly terms and who took part in his 1769 Shakespeare festival, lived at The Cedars, the house which David Garrick obtained for his nephew David Garrick, who lived there from ca. 1780 till his death in 1795, and who is commemorated in the present name of the house, Garrick's House. There also came to Hampton James Coutts and Sir Richard Carr Glyn, both well known bankers, the former at Hill House, which was demolished in 1902 to make way for the filter beds in Station Road, and the latter at Castle House (Fig 10). General James Johnstone, one time Governor of Quebec, lived at Spring Grove from 1784 to ca. 1792 and then moved to Castle House, where his widow continued to live after his death in 1798. In 1823 Castle House became the home of the Jackson and Kent families for upwards of 100 years. General Johnstone was succeeded at Spring Grove by John Greg, a prosperous sugar planter from Dominica, whose tomb is such a prominent feature of the churchyard. In 1796 the 5th Duke of St Albans, great grandson of Charles II and Nell Gwynne, came to live at the house by the river later named St Albans Bank and later still St Albans. Most noted of all, the Duke of Clarence came to live at Bushy Lodge in 1797 with his mistress, the actress Dorothea Jordan, and the house was populated by their ten children for many years afterwards, even after the Duke had brought his Duchess, Princess Adelaide of Saxe Meiningen, to live there in 1819.

Sir Archibald Edmonstone, the first baronet, lived at the Brick House (now Grove House) from 1782 until 1801, when he made it over to his fourth son, Neil Benjamin, who spent much of his life in India, firstly as official Persian translator, then as Secretary to the Viceroy. Neil Benjamin Edmonstone had a great influence on Lord Wellesley in the development of East India Company rule over India. During his absence in India Grove House was occupied by his eldest brother, Sir Charles, who succeeded his father in 1807. On the death of Sir Thomas Frederick in 1770 the Manor House estate passed to his daughters Elizabeth, who later married Sir John Morshead, and Selina, who became Mrs Robert Thistlethwayte. From ca. 1800 to 1814 they let it to Baron Hotham, a Baron of the Exchequer, about whom it was said that his knowledge of the law was very scanty. Sir Charles Edmonstone and his wife, who was Baron Hotham's daughter, then moved across the road from Grove House to the Manor House. In 1820, when both of Sir Thomas Frederick's daughters had died, parts of the estate were sold. After Sir Charles Edmonstone's death his widow lived there until 1832, when Lady Goodricke bought the Manor House with the farmhouse. On her death she left the estate to her solicitor, Mr G. F. Barlow, who in turn sold it to the Earl of Carlisle, in whose hands it remained until it was broken up for housing development at the turn of the century.

In 1799 Captain the Hon. George Grey, a Commissioner of the Royal Navy, bought what remained of a house built by the great organist and composer, John Blow, about 1690, and was granted permission to demolish it. The site was sold by him to Lady Ann Sheridan, widow of Sir Henry Sheridan, the fourth baronet, in 1804. Lady Ann died in 1808 and a subsequent owner at some time before 1825 built a house called Rose Villa, now known as Beveree. For a short time it was rented by Edward Jesse, sometime Deputy Surveyor of Royal Parks and Palaces and a writer on natural history.

The group of houses known as Riverdale, on the site now occupied by the Riverdale works of the Metropolitan Water Board, had some notable owners. William Wightman, later a well known Queen's Bench judge, lived there ca. 1811 – 1820, and returned to Hampton some years later to live at St Albans. Another resident of Riverdale from 1815 to 1821, Henry Fauntleroy, achieved notoriety as the last man to be hanged in England for forgery. The Rt Revd Dr Robert Stanser, second Bishop of Nova Scotia, lived here from 1817 until his death in 1829.

In the year 1800 Hampton's upper crust was composed largely of widows. Mrs Eva Garrick was at Hampton House, Mrs Charlotte Beard at Rose Hill, and Mrs Greg at Spring Grove. The widow of David Garrick the nephew married again and lived at The Cedars until about 1801. Mrs Ann Hare was at the house now forming Park and Barham Houses. At Elm Lodge there was Mrs Gouldsmith, the widow of a prosperous London merchant, and another widow, Mrs Elizabeth Glover, was living at the large house which formerly stood where Staplegrove (No. 6 Church Street) now stands. This house was always referred to in the Court Rolls as "the house of Edward Wood", who appears to have achieved no great distinction and in any case lived there for but a short time at the beginning of the eighteenth century. The house of Edward Wood was bought from Mrs Glover in 1803 by Noel Desenfans, who came from Douai as a teacher of French, became a well known connoisseur of pictures, and by his bequests was instrumental in founding the Dulwich College Art Gallery. On his death in 1807 he bequeathed the house to Elizabeth Glover, after whose death it was bought by a John Bent, who demolished it in ca. 1818 and built the present Staplegrove, Hemming Lodge, Chelwood, Almond House and Rosemary House on the land.

The village surgeon and apothecary, William James Griffinhoofe, lived at the house later known as Cranham House and then The Moorings. Dr Griffinhoofe's practice was taken by David Davis, who had attended the Duchess of Kent at the birth of Queen Victoria. The house was used as a doctor's house until nearly the end of the century, firstly by Dr T. H. Holberton and then by his son, Dr Vaughan Holberton. The second apothecary in the village, Mr Maurice Jones, lived firstly at the Old Grange and then at Lion House (No. 3 Thames Street) until ca. 1816. Dr Henry Jepson came to Hampton in 1823, living first at Orme House and then at the house now called Riverdale (No. 1 Thames Street) from 1832 until his death in 1887.

LOCAL GOVERNMENT – THE MANOR COURT AND THE VESTRY

In 1800 almost the whole of Hampton was still held by copyhold of the Lord of the Manor of Hampton Court, namely the King. The jurisdiction of the Lord was exercised in theory by his Chief Steward, but in practice by the Deputy Steward, who presided over meetings of the "homage" or jury consisting of up to fifteen of the copyholders. The Manor Court met annually at about Easter to mark its allegiance to the Lord and to deal with court business, sitting firstly as a Court Leet and then as a Court Baron. The Court Leet dealt with such matters as encroachments, the maintenance of fences and ditches, unauthorized grazing, and the maintenance of the pound. It also elected for the year following a Constable and his deputy or Headborough, one each for the Town and the Wick. By 1800 the Court Leet's activities were confined to the appointment of constables and headboroughs.

The Court Baron was concerned with the transfer of copyhold property from one customary tenant to another by inheritance, sale or mortgage, and with the occasional granting of a plot of common land on copyhold tenure. The latter function ceased with the allotment of common land under the Enclosure Act of 1811, but the Court Baron was still concerned with all subsequent transactions as long as the property remained copyhold. From about 1830 tenants were allowed to enfranchise their copyholds so that by the end of the century the Court Baron had much less to do. Many of the transactions were performed out of court by the Deputy Steward, and the Court Baron expired in 1936.

By 1800 local administration, apart from the appointment of constable and headborough, was in the hands of the Vestry, that is to say, of all parishioners paying rates. Whenever a matter of sufficient importance required a decision, the Vestry would be assembled, but in practice almost all of the administration was undertaken by the parish officers, the Churchwardens, Overseers of the Poor and Surveyors of Highways, who were elected at the annual general meeting at Easter. The Vestry Clerk and the Beadle, who were responsible for giving effect to the decisions of the Vestry or of the parish officers, were normally elected for longer periods. National control of the Vestry was exercised through the Justices of the Peace, who had to approve the appointment of the parish officers.

The Vestry was responsible for church maintenance, relief of the poor, upkeep of the roads, and other matters which during the first half of the century included vagrancy, the control of public houses, maintenance of the fire engine, drainage and flood protection, the provision of militia substitutes and, in a rudimentary way, the health of the parish, especially during the cholera epidemic of 1832. In 1811 the Vestry was gravely concerned at the "depraved state of morals evidenced in the improper behaviour and indecent langauge of the youth of this parish" and ordered the beadle to take into custody all young persons playing at games in the streets on Sundays or at any time using indecent or profane language.

A spate of robberies in 1812 caused the Vestry to establish a nightly watch. Three watch boxes fitted with alarm bells were set up and watchmen were appointed to patrol the streets. It was then decided to form an association of parishioners to patrol the streets to see that the watchmen were doing their job and were sober. The watch seems to have been effective, for the scheme was abandoned shortly afterwards. It was revived in earnest in 1828, when it was reported that "many robberies have lately been perpetrated in the dwellings and outhouses of the inhabitants and attempts have been made to steal corpses from the churchyard and burial ground". On this occasion the watch was kept up for nearly two years and was not abandoned until some time after the conviction of the notorious Edinburgh body-snatchers, Burke and Hare.

Hampton being a Royal parish, the Vestry was often concerned with manifestations of loyalty. In 1809 a celebration of the beginning of the 50th year of the reign of George III was organized. A subscription was raised and food and drink were given to the poor, each adult receiving 1½ lb of meat, a quartern loaf and a quart of beer, and each child ½ lb of meat, half a quartern loaf and half a pint of beer. The surplus money was used later to supply the poor with clothing, coal and soap. A service was held in church on the day, 25 October 1809, after which "the greater part of the respectable inhabitants of the parish dined together at the Bell Inn and spent and concluded the day in perfect harmony with each other and in demonstrations of loyalty and attachment to their venerated Monarch and the Invaluable Constitution of their country".

On the death of George III the Vestry expressed to the new king "their zealous attachment to the Throne and determination to defend that glorious Constitution which your Majesty has so steadily and powerfully maintained" and observed "with the deepest concern and regret the base and insidious acts by which a wicked and unprincipled faction has endeavoured to delude the credulous and unwary and through the means of licentious and blasphemous publications to overturn the altar and the throne".

The death of George IV and accession of William IV were marked by a specially unctuous address to the new King and Queen as parishioners of Hampton. This was presented in person in the drawing room at Bushy House by the Vicar, Curate, Churchwardens, Vestry Clerk and twenty selected inhabitants. The King and Queen later went into the Hall to meet those for whom there had been no room and thanked them in a "most gracious and condescending manner". Seven years later the parish presented an address of condolence to Queen Adelaide on the death of William IV, but there appears to have been no formal address of loyalty to Queen Victoria.

Every seventh year, on Ascension Day, the Vestry organized the centuries-old custom of perambulating the parish boundaries, commonly called beating the bounds. This took place regularly from 1802 to 1893. Then for some reason there was a break with custom and the next one took place on 7 July 1898. The last full-scale one took place on Ascension Day in 1905.

The bounds were usually followed in an anti-clockwise direction, starting from Bell Hill, down the river to Hampton Court and round the south and east fronts of the Palace, over the wall into Tennis Court Lane, along the back of the barrack block and the inside of the wall facing Vrow Walk, over the wall into the road to Kingston, into No. 1 Park Side and out through the kitchen window into Bushy Park, where there would be a pause for refreshments under a chestnut tree, then parallel with the Chestnut Avenue and by a tortuous route to Teddington Corner where a service was held based on the text from Deuteronomy "Cursed is he that removeth his neighbour's landmark". The party then continued via Burton's Lane to the Hounslow Road, now Uxbridge Road, where another stop was made for refreshment, over to Donkey Hall at the end of Hanworth Long Lane (Oak Avenue) and southward beside Kempton Park to the River Thames and so back to Bell Hill and a rollicking dinner at the Red Lion or the Bell.

SOCIAL WELFARE

The Workhouse

Organized parochial help for the poor, as distinct from the haphazard foundation and allocation of charities, derived from an Act of 1601 which called for the appointment of up to three Overseers of the Poor in each parish. Hampton had two overseers who for the most part, made allocations to those who were living in their own houses, but from about 1723 to 1770 some of those in need were cared for in a poor house known as the Cross House, which stood near to where the White Hart is now. The Cross House had been a small farmhouse before it was rented by the parish. In 1770 the Vestry resolved to build a new poor house or workhouse on the common and the Cross House was bought by the Earl of Pomfret who sold it to David Garrick in 1775, the site being known as Pomfret Paddock for many years afterwards.

The new workhouse was built in the apex formed by the Hanworth and Uxbridge Roads at a cost of £400. The money was to have been lent by Sir Thomas Frederick at 4 per cent interest, but he died in 1770 and Mr Stephen Wise lent the money at 5 per cent interest. When he agreed to do this he can have had little idea that it would take the parish 58 years to repay the loan to his descendants.

No picture or plan of the workhouse is known to exist, but documentary evidence shows that it was built of brick, with a tiled roof, and that there was a hall, committee room, pest room, rooms for the master and his family, and six bedrooms to accommodate up to 40 persons. Each bedroom had three feather beds and it was rarely necessary for more than two to sleep in a bed. Hygiene was catered for by the provision of vinegar "for preventing infectious scent" and spirits of turpentine for killing vermin in the beds. The importance of cleanliness was recognized and regulations drawn up in 1800 required the master to see that the poor were cleanly and decent in their persons, that the workhouse was swept clean every morning and washed once a week at least, and that clean body and bed linen were provided. The regulations also specified the food and drink to be provided in the following terms:

> Boiled Clods, Stickings, Leg of Mutton Peices (sic), Legs or Cheeks of Ox Beef — Bread of the Household Kind — Pease or other Soup made after the Method prescribed by the Charitable Societies — Vegetables and Roots — Milk — Milk Pottage — Rice Milk — Water Gruel — Cheese — Butter — Small Beer to the making of which one Bushel and a half of Malt shall at the least be allowed to a Barrel of 36 Gallons — Candles — Soap and other Necessaries for washing Linen — and Fuel for Firing.

Breakfast was to be provided at 8 a.m., dinner at 1 p.m. and supper at 7 p.m. The able-bodied poor were to be employed on domestic duties within the boundaries of the workhouse, including the cultivation of the 2-acre garden to provide vegetables.

Hampton's workhouse seems to have been unusual in that the records contain no complaints of harsh treatment. Sir Frederick Eden inspected the workhouse in 1795 and reported that the food seemed wholesome and was certainly better than a labouring man could afford for his family. Sir Frederick also noted that the female paupers would have been riotous without their morning tea, even though this was against the rules.

The administration of the workhouse was at first supervised by a small committee appointed by the Vestry, but in 1819 a Select Vestry consisting of twenty substantial householders (including the Duke of Clarence) was appointed annually to comply with an Act of Parliament. From time to time the Hampton workhouse also cared for the poor of Hampton Wick and Teddington, the intention being that an additional charge would be made to enable the building debt to be paid off. On the passing of the Amendment of the Poor Law Act (1834) Hampton, Hampton Wick, and Teddington joined with a number of parishes in Surrey to form the Kingston Union. The new Board of Guardians decided to close the Hampton workhouse on Lady Day 1837 and to transfer the inmates to Kingston. Life in the workhouse there was more spartan than it had been at Hampton and the Board frequently had to censure the master and mistress for their harsh conduct. The Hampton Vestry tried to dispose of the workhouse as soon as possible, but did not receive permission until 1846, whereupon the building was demolished.

Almshouses

A row of six small thatched almshouses was built in 1723. They stood just to the north of the present ones and were in use until 1895 although by 1868 they were said to be so dilapidated as to be unfit for human habitation. In 1887 it was decided that the best way of permanently celebrating Queen Victoria's Golden Jubilee would be to build new almshouses, and a fund was started for the purpose. The response, however, proved inadequate and it was not until 1895 that a donation of £100 by Mr Auguste de Wette made it possible for them to be built. On the occasion of the opening by Mrs de Wette on 2 April 1895 the Surrey Comet described them in the following terms:

> "The structure is after the early English style of architecture . . . The lower part is faced with red brick-work and the gables and upper part is rough-cast work in white spar, having tastily designed cement framework . . . The upper portions of the windows are lead-glazed with cathedral tinted glass and the roof is covered with alternate bands of plain and ornamental Borseley tiles of different shades. The gable boards are of ornamental pattern, as are also the posts supporting the roofs and porches."

The Charities

Over the years those in need have benefitted from bequests of five or ten pounds too numerous to mention. The larger bequests in being before 1800 were:

Mary Oram (1676) – £50 to purchase land to provide rent to be used for the apprenticeship of poor children. To this end Holly Bush Close was bought in 1678.

Mary Gavell (1746) – £100 to earn interest to provide bread for the poor of Hampton, but none for the Wick, and £5 for a board to hold the bread.

John Turner (1753) – £500 – the interest to be divided among six poor women.

Cyrus Maigre (1777) – £100 – the interest to be used to buy bread.

Other benefactions by Robert Hammond (1557), Edmund Pigeon (1657) and John Jones (1692) were primarily for the benefit of the Free Grammar School, but John Jones provided also for the payment of £6 a year to "six aged and poor men who are of good life and conversation".

The first benefaction of the nineteenth century was that of

William Cole – £1000 – to provide a handsome board commemorating himself and the interest on the remainder to be given to the poor who did not receive parish relief.

From the account of a meeting of parishioners in 1807 it is clear that there was dissatisfaction at the way in which the charities were being administered and it was resolved that a proper account of the distribution of the income should be kept and that the bequests of John Jones, John Turner, Cyrus Maigre and William Cole, and other minor bequests, should be amalgamated. Other bequests received during the 19th century included:

Mrs Eva Garrick (1822) – £300 – the interest to provide coal for the poor.

W. M. Chinnery (1880) late of Rose Hill – £100 for the poor with priority for the occupants of the almshouses.

Another bequest, though not for the poor, was that of James Annett (1834) who left £700 to provide remuneration for the bellringers of the parish church to ring a peal every Sunday morning between the hours of ten and eleven.

The Coal Charity arose from the Enclosure Award when 10 acres of land on the northern boundary of the parish (and also 5 acres for Hampton Wick) were allocated for the benefit of the poor in compensation for the loss by them of the right of gathering fuel on the common.

The charities were reviewed again in 1816, when Mr William Jackson produced an authoritative list of them, and again in 1835. In 1864 the Charity Commissioners held an inquiry into Hampton's charities, but this was mainly concerned with the School charities and is dealt with elsewhere. It was not until 1891 that the Charity Commissioners held an inquiry with the aim of establishing a comprehensive scheme for the administration of all of Hampton's charities. By the application of delaying tactics the parishioners succeeded in having the adoption of the scheme postponed until November 1894, when eight Parochial Charity Trustees were elected, four for Hampton and four for Hampton Hill.

Benefit Societies

It was early recognized that one of the best forms of welfare was the formation of societies for the encouragement of thrift. As early as 1810 a Female Friendly Society was formed whereby, for an entrance fee of half-a-crown and a quarterly payment of 3s., provision would be made for the expenses of confinement, sickness and death. A White Hart Friendly Society was founded in 1838 and flourished until 1912 when the coming into effect of Lloyd George's National Insurance Act made it no longer necessary. Perhaps the greatest boon was the foundation of the Hampton Co-operative Society in a small room in Milton Road in 1879. The society prospered and was soon able to open the still existing shop in Station Road. Another boon was the foundation of the East and West Moulsey, Hampton and Thames Ditton Permanent Building Society on 23 April 1852 mainly through the initiative of Mr F. J. Kent sen.

Philanthropy

The Hampton Philanthropic Society was founded in 1875 by Robert Lawrence, who had the butcher's shop at No. 22 High Street, and it is still active after nearly a hundred years. Allied organizations were a Clothing Club and a Blanket Loan Society which for many years in the 1860s and 1870s used to lend blankets to those in need at the beginning of November and recover them the following May. In the 1880s Mrs Archer, of Hill House, founded a Winter Work Society for poor women. In 1881 Mrs J. P. Kitchin, of the Manor House, conscious of the lack of a meeting place for working men other than the public houses, took the lease of a house at the Triangle (later known as Germany's grocery store and now as Champion's Pantry) and had it converted for this purpose, calling it the Welcome Coffee House. It had a brightly decorated coffee room, a smoking room and reading room with newspapers, books and games, and a tea garden. Meals were provided at very modest prices and families could have their meals cooked there for a penny a time. Rather surprisingly it was closed for lack of support in 1891, but was opened again in 1892 and was very much appreciated when so many men were thrown out of work by the great frosts of 1893 and 1895.

RECREATION

What organized recreation there was of the sporting type at the start of the century took place on Moulsey Hurst. Hampton Races were run there and, although they were sometimes described as the Cockney Derby, were often attended by the nobility and sometimes by royalty, especially after William IV raised their status by providing a £100 prize for one of the races. It was often said that the races were a matter of indifference to those attending, whose main interest was the booths, side-shows and general revelry. The police were hard put to it to keep order and indeed failed to do so at the June meeting of 1845 when "300 – 400 gipsies and other low and desperate characters" severely beat three policemen and threw them into the river. Fortunately help was near at hand and they were rescued. The old-style Hampton Races took place for the last time in 1887, but some two years later the Hurst Park Club was founded and racing continued until the 1960s, when the racecourse was sold and developed as a housing estate.

Molesey Hurst was the scene of many a prize fight. Henry Ripley in his "History of Hampton-upon-Thames" quotes graphic descriptions of a number of these. On 8 December 1818, for example, Scroggins and Martin "pummelled one another into a state of stupor nearly" and on 24 October 1820 Martin went one better when he "pounded David Hudson's face out of all resemblance to humanity". The violence did not end with the fight and it was said that the streets of Hampton resounded with drunken orgies until the small hours.

As far as cricket was concerned Molesey Hurst ranked with Hambledon and for many years some of the best teams used to play there. Hampton's first cricket club, the Clarence, was founded under the active patronage of the Duke of Clarence and had its pitch on the Hurst. The Clarence Club had many ups and downs and ceased to exist in the 1870s. In 1881, however, a new Clarence Club was formed. In time the name Clarence was dropped and the home ground was moved to Bushy Park, near to the north-western entrance to the Watergate plantation.

The playing of football of a sort in the streets was for long a tradition on Shrove Tuesday, but in 1864 authority forcibly showed its disapproval.

For many fishing was a matter of necessity, but the interests of the sporting fisherman were uppermost when the Thames Angling Preservation Society was formed at a meeting at the Bell Inn in 1838. The society ran a hatchery in a meadow near the Sunbury boundary and from 1864 onwards released large numbers of fish into the Thames. Hamptonians started to derive recreation from the river in 1835, when the Watermen's Regatta was first held. The events included serious racing and some frivolous antics such as water jousting and pillow fighting and the regatta was held annually until 1910. A Rowing Club was formed in 1871 and held regattas for a number of years; and as long ago as 1870 Hampton Grammar School started to make its name as a rowing school.

Organized sailing started with the formation of the Thames Valley Sailing Club in 1876. The club had its headquarters at Hampton and club races and matches were held throughout the season until well into the new century. In the last twenty years of the century the river also provided a highly favoured form of passive recreation in the form of an outing on one of the new launches built at Hampton.

The exclusive Garrick Lawn Tennis Club was formed in 1883 and used courts at Garrick's Villa by permission of Mrs Grove. The membership was limited to fifty and election was by ballot of the existing members. Perhaps in reply to some adverse criticism the Vicar, as President, wrote "this is a game indulged in more by the rich than the poor, yet as those whom God has blessed with riches in this our parish of Hampton are, for the most part, ready to use these when occasion arises for the benefit of the poor, so they will not grudge this kind effort to give their richer friends and neighbours an opportunity much wanted of meeting on common ground for a most popular and health-giving recreation."

The Hampton Working Men's Club and Institute was responsible for the formation of two of Hampton's most popular clubs, the Harriers, founded in 1889, and the Cycling Club founded in 1891. Members of both of these clubs achieved successes in county and national championships and became popular heroes. When a new ferry boat was launched in 1906 it was named "Beale" after one of the Harriers' champion athletes.

The Venison Dinner

The first evidence of organized social contact between the inhabitants is in reports of what was at first called the November the Fifth Dinner, later known as the Venison Dinner when the Duke of Clarence provided a Bushy Park buck for it. It was always held at the Red Lion and was essentially a tradesmen's affair. Apart from the customary toasts there were two traditional ones "Prosperity to the Town and Trade of Hampton" and "Success to the roof we are under". It was no event for the gentry and it was not until 1875 that the Vicar attended, "giving it a stamp of respectability". It will never be known whether this had any connection with its ceasing to be held after 1878, apart from one revival in 1886.

Entertainment was based on the home and the ability of families to amuse themselves. Even so the Vestry in 1828 resolved to prohibit dancing and drinking in private houses. The first attempt at cultural association was in 1853 when a Literary Society was formed to provide a reading room and lending library and to hold conversaziones and lectures. All seemed to be going well when the Vicar, the Revd Edward Johnstone, the society's first chairman, resigned in a huff because the committee decided to have its printing done by a tradesman with whom he was in dispute. From all accounts it would have been difficult to find one with whom he was not in dispute. Dr T. H. Holberton was then elected chairman, but on his sudden death in 1855 the society collapsed.

A Choral Society formed in 1866 gave a few concerts with assistance from the Kingston Choral Society, but lasted for only two or three years. Another choral society was formed in the 1890s, but this too had only a brief existence. This did not mean, however, that Hampton was musically barren. Concerts by local amateurs were a regular feature from the 1860s onwards, usually as a means of raising money for a good cause. With our hindsight, however, we can be critical of the commonest way of raising money for the relatives of those who had died young from respiratory and circulatory diseases – the holding of a smoking concert.

All along Hampton Hill seems to have been more enterprising than Hampton in organizing cultural pursuits. Penny Readings with musical interludes were held there as early as 1865. Hampton followed about a year later and penny readings were well supported in both districts until 1880 or so. The national craze for spelling bees was indulged in at Hampton Hill for some time before it struck Hampton. Also Hampton Hill started a Lecture and Debating Society which served both areas very successfully for many years after.

An occasional ball was organized in Hampton as early as 1857. These were held in the English School Room and it seems a little surprising to read that in 1858 "the merry dance was kept up with unflagging spirit until 6 o'clock in the morning". Towards the end of the century many more balls were held and it was normal for dancing to continue until the milkman was on his way round.

The Flower Show was the great occasion of the year in which all could join. Again the lead was taken by Hampton Hill. The first show was organized for cottagers by the Working Men's Club in September 1872. By 1875 two shows were being held in each year, but it was not until 1879 that Hampton joined in and the society was named the Hampton and New Hampton Horticultural and Cottage Garden Society ("New Hampton" being replaced by "Hampton Hill" in 1882). The first show to be held in Hampton took place in July 1881 in the grounds of Garrick's Villa. It was still essentially a working man's flower show, but after Princess Frederica of Hanover, who with her husband lived at Hampton Court Palace, agreed to become patroness of it and sometimes presented the prizes, well-to-do Hamptonians found it attractive and it became an occasion for the whole village. From 1883 onwards the show was held in the Manor House grounds at Hampton and the Vicarage meadow at Hampton Hill alternately.

TRADES AND OCCUPATIONS

As has already been observed, Hampton at the beginning of the century was looked on as a resort where some of London's well-to-do had their country homes. At that time the majority of the inhabitants gained a livelihood by serving the gentry and one another by providing necessities such as food and drink, clothing, lighting in the form of candles, house building and maintenance, and the care of two surgeon-apothecaries and a midwife. By 1840 a chemist was in business where the pharmacy is today at No. 10 High Street. The number of servants living in was not recorded in the earlier census returns, but in 1841 there were, for example, nine servants and a governess living at Rose Hill, and in 1851 there were twelve servants at St. Albans Bank and eleven at Garrick's Villa; and the Vicar of the day had six.

Some of Hampton's income from outside was derived from travellers using the ten inns and some from the private education referred to later. Trades which served a wider area included candle making at the factory in Thames Street, the culture of osiers and the making of baskets, straw hat and stay making, the making of bricks, and the sale of gravel from the pits on the common after the parish's own requirements had been met.

A substantial part of Hampton (and all of Hampton Hill) was still common land at the time of the Enclosure Act. Of the remaining area part took the form of smallholdings in the tenure of the owners of the larger houses, probably used for the grazing of carriage horses and the raising of a few cattle, kine and fowl for food. The remainder was farmed by three or four farmers. In 1823 and 1841 there was just one market gardener. An important feature of the latter part of the century was the growth of market gardening at the expense of farming. Although the prospects for market gardening were greatly improved by the rapid railway communication with London after 1863, it was not until the 1880s that the trade began to flourish. In 1884 there was still only one nursery; by 1888 there were twelve and by 1900 there were thirty-two, with about 600 greenhouses. The trade continued to grow and there were still 45 nurseries in business in 1939, but with the ever growing demand for land for building, what used to be Hampton's main landmark has largely disappeared and now, in 1973, there are no more than eight.

The nurseries attracted many workers from Germany, France and Belgium in the 1890s and even a few from Russia and Austria. Some of them took back their experience to their home countries; some went on to the United States; and quite a number stayed in Hampton. In the 1890s large quantities of grapes, tomatoes, cucumbers, strawberries, mushrooms, melons, early potatoes and French beans were grown, but the production of flowers exceeded that of fruit and vegetables.

The other big development which took much of the farming land and provided employment arose from the passing of an Act in 1852 prohibiting water companies from taking water from the tidal reaches of the Thames. Within a short space of time three companies, the

Grand Junction, Southwark and Vauxhall, and West Middlesex had taken over a large part of the riverside fields, and had erected their plants by 1855. To meet the ever growing demand the companies expanded their works from time to time, the biggest changes being the construction of the Stain Hill reservoir and the Riverdale Works in the 1890s and the excavation of the Station Road filter beds in 1902. At each of these stages there was much indignation at the spoliation of Hampton's scenery and when the Riverdale works were built one protester said that no other civilized country would allow such vandalism. However, with the vital need for a supply of safe drinking water, Hampton had to bow to the inevitable, and the most that could be hoped for was the successful outcome of the campaign by Middlesex County Councillor Auguste de Wette for the preservation of a riverside walk beside the water companies' property, but this was not to be.

By the 1870s boat building had become established and before long achieved an international reputation. Messrs. Tagg supplied boats of high quality that were used in many parts of the world, as too were the electric launches of Messrs Immisch & Co. of Platt's Eyot, the predecessors of Messrs Thorneycroft.

In 1890 the cabinet works of Messrs Farmer was started in Avenue Road and before long the manufacture of copying apparatus called the Copy Cat was undertaken. The candle factory in Thames Street had taken up the manufacture of Volvolutum soap and incurred the wrath of the neighbours by the emission of offensive smells. These complaints culminated in proceedings brought against the owners by the Local Board, involving the expenditure of £430 of the parishioners' money with very little to show for it. A sign of the times was the setting up of a bicycle factory and repair service in Red Lion Square by Messrs Kingsbury & Son. By 1900 Hampton had its first bank, Ashby's, on the site of the present Barclays bank at the corner of Station Road and High Street.

SCHOOLS

The Grammar School

From 1726 onwards the Hampton Free Grammar School occupied the room adjoining the new north aisle of the church. The Master from 1791 to 1803 was the Revd Richard Kilsha, who does not appear to have been very assiduous in his duties. His successor was elected according to custom by the vote of all parishioners paying scot and lot, the equivalent of the modern ratepayers. The election of a new schoolmaster was an event which caused as much interest locally as a Parliamentary election. Polling took place in the school room from 10 a.m. to 3 p.m., when the counting of the votes started. On this occasion the successful candidate was the Revd Samuel Hemming, who became well known as the founder of the Hemming Masonic Lodge. The Revd Dr Hemming was an ebullient man who was frequently in dispute with the School Trustees. At a meeting on 9 July 1828 the Trustees went so far as to record their opinion that "the Duties of the Master of the Free School of this Parish have for a long Series of Years past (and especially during the respective Masterships of the late Dr Hemming and his immediate predecessor the Revd Mr Kilsha) been grossly abused and neglected in as much as the Tuition of the Scholars has been chiefly intrusted to Assistant Teachers who were engaged by the Masters at a low Salary, and who did not possess adequate Ability to discharge the Functions of their Office."

The plan for rebuilding St Mary's church, referred to later, required the demolition of the old schoolroom. Although the Vestry resolved in 1828 to give the building of a new schoolroom priority over the building of a new church, no action was taken and when the fabric of the old church was pulled down in 1830, the school was homeless. Some consideration had already been given to a new site and it had been decided in principle that the new school should be in two parts, a Latin or Upper School and an English or Lower School with quarters for an under Master, but there was a shortage of money and the only way in which sufficient funds could be raised was to allow the endowment income to accumulate for a few years. Although no new Master was appointed on the death of Dr Hemming in 1828, some form of elementary education was carried on, though exactly where is not known, under Mr George Bridges who was able to satisfy the Trustees that he could write and do arithmetic and was appointed acting Master at a salary of £1 5s. a week. Although the Trustees expressed themselves as highly satisfied with Mr Bridges, they found with regret that, as a result of the neglect by Mr Kilsha and Dr Hemming, the only children being sent to the school were those of persons in the lowest rank who could not afford to pay for their instruction elsewhere. Nevertheless, the Trustees would accept only the children of those who paid rates and resolved to dismiss boys who behaved disorderly or contumaciously.

Almost five years elapsed between the demolition of the old schoolroom and the building of the new school on the site of the present parish hall. The new building had a wing at the north end for the Latin School and another at the south end for the English School and in between was a two-storeyed apartment for the under Master. Mr Bridges continued in charge until 1839 when it was decided to appoint a new Master. The election caused, if anything, greater excitement than any previous election of a Master, and was reported in The Times. The candidates were the Revd H. R. Slade, curate of St Mary's since 1835, and the Revd Robert Peel. The election was conducted on unashamedly partisan lines and the candidates adopted symbolic colours, the Reds or Conservatives supporting Mr Peel and the Blues or Radicals supporting Mr Slade. On this occasion the polling hours were from 9 a.m. until 6 p.m. and the Revd Robert Peel was elected by 357 votes to his opponent's 272.

The division of the Grammar School into a Latin School and an English School did not prove as satisfactory as was expected. The middle class parents, on whom the Latin School largely depended, gradually withdrew their support, probably because they did not wish their sons to have too much contact with their social inferiors.

It seems clear too that Mr Peel did not give the school his best attention as he grew older. By 1858 the numbers had fallen to such an extent that the Charity Commissioners ordered an inquiry, which in the event did not take place until 1864. In the intervening period Mr Francis had been appointed Master of the English School and through his exertions had brought the number of scholars up to 120. The Surrey Comet reported the twice-yearly treats given to the school by Mr F. J. Kent the younger and it is probably significant that, whereas Mr Peel's name was not mentioned, fulsome praise was lavished on Mr Francis.

The Charity Commissioners' new scheme was not announced until December 1866. Its main feature was the payment of 3d a week for each boy or 4d a week for two brothers. This caused great indignation and parishioners were not slow to point out that Hammond, Pigeon and John Jones had endowed the school so that it might be free. A committee of tradesmen was formed in March 1867 to fight the scheme and a formal protest was sent to the Charity Commissioners, who merely replied that the scheme had been established and it was not in their power to alter it. The committee replied with another protest, but it was to no avail and Mr Francis (apparently acting for Mr Peel) had to say at the beginning of the summer term that he could not teach any boy who had not paid his weekly fee. Mr F. O. Martin, of Rose Hill, provided tickets for 21 of the poorer boys, but they tore these up and there arose the bizarre situation of boys trying to force their way into school. It was only when the police arrived that they agreed to forgo their lessons. Still the protesters did not give in and in February 1868 they applied to the Court of Chancery for an injunction to restrain the Trustees from applying the scheme. The protest had by now, however, lost most of its steam; the injunction was refused; and the new scheme was quietly accepted.

Mr Peel resigned late in 1866 or early in 1867, presumably on grounds of ill health for he died shortly afterwards, and a new Headmaster was appointed to the Latin School, which then had only nine pupils. This was the Revd G. F. Heather, who put all his energy into building up the school. The numbers grew steadily and before long the Trustees obtained Jessamine House in Thames Street to provide a home for Mr Heather and for a few boarders. A second master was appointed and the curriculum was expanded to include French and German. The Grammar School had a Rugby football team by 1874 and the first athletic sports took place in 1875. There was now talk in earnest about building a new school and a site was chosen in the Upper Sunbury Road which had been allocated to the Vicar under the Enclosure Award in lieu of tithes. To raise money for the building it was decided to sell the vicarage meadow on the opposite side of the road, the income from which was John Jones' bequest. There was a ready purchaser in the shape of the Grand Junction Water Company who paid £10,500 for the land. The sale of this charity land to raise money for building a school for the sons of gentlemen caused predictable indignation in certain quarters, but a public meeting welcomed the proposal.

The new school was intended to take 100 dayboys and 50 boarders and fees for dayboys whose parents had resided in Hampton for at least three years were to be not less than £8 and not more than £12 a year. The foundation stone was laid by Lord George Hamilton on 11 October 1879 and the new school was ready for occupation the following July.

It must have been a great grief to Mr Heather to have to witness a steady fall in the number of boys attending the new school whose future had seemed so bright. For various reasons dealt with by Garside in his "Brief History of Hampton School" there were no more than 39 boys by 1892 and as few as 28 by 1897. The Charity Commissioners ordered an enquiry and put forward a new scheme involving greater representation on the governing body by the Urban District and County Councils and a reduction in the number of co-opted governors, a foretaste of the Education Act of 1902. With the appointment of Mr W. A. Roberts as Headmaster in 1897 the tide soon began to turn, however, and by 1906 the number of boys had risen to nearly 200.

Fig. 1. The Old Church of St Mary, demolished in 1829

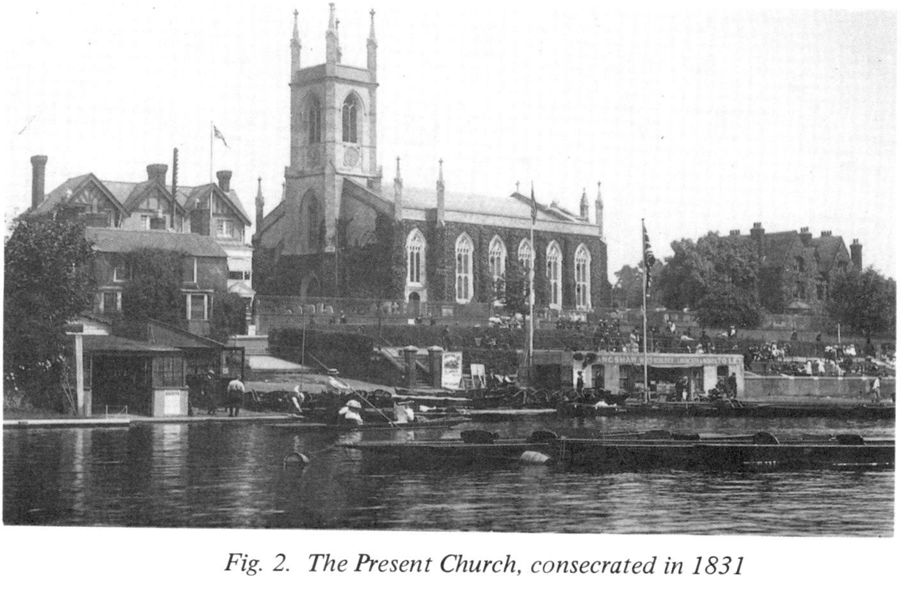

Fig. 2. The Present Church, consecrated in 1831

Fig. 3. View c. 1860 looking towards "The Feathers"

Fig. 4. The "Old" Bell Hotel, destroyed by fire in 1892

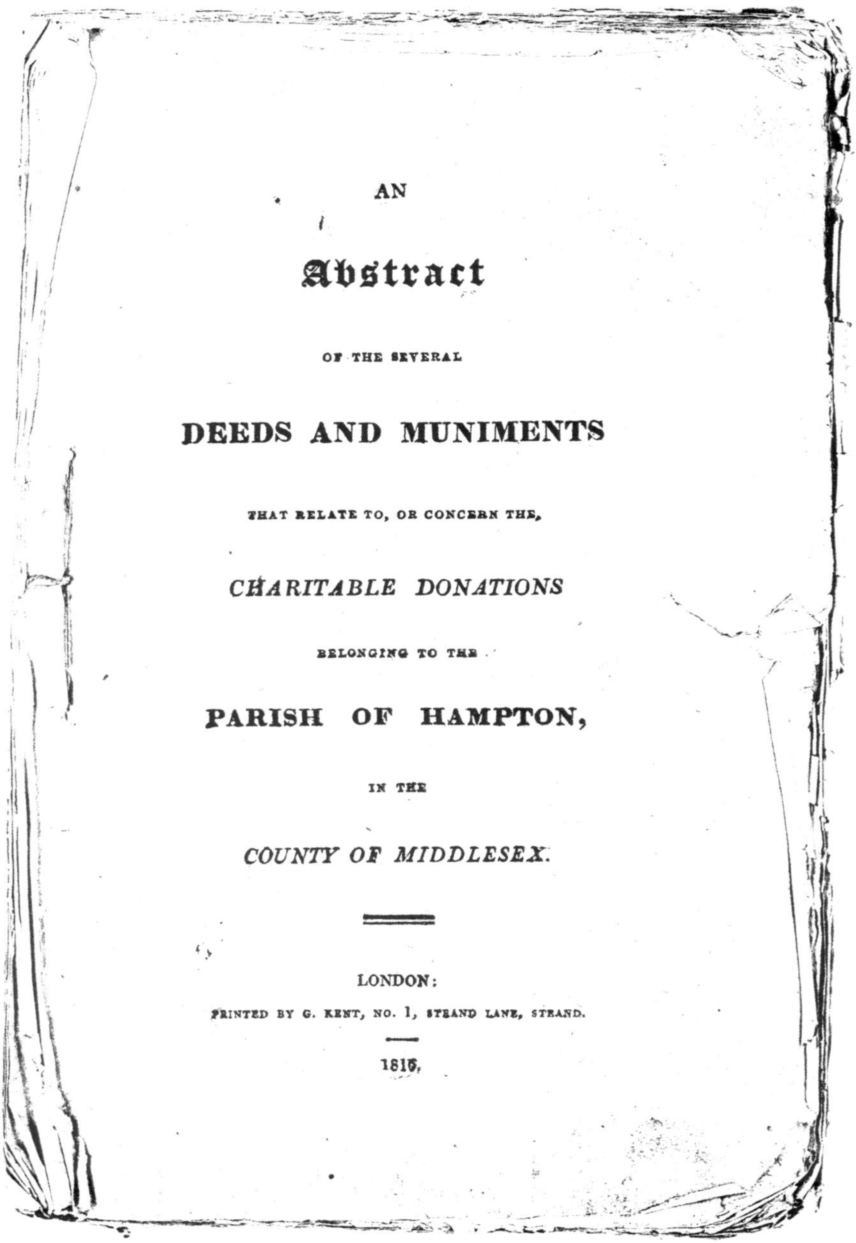

AN

Abstract

OF THE SEVERAL

DEEDS AND MUNIMENTS

THAT RELATE TO, OR CONCERN THE,

CHARITABLE DONATIONS

BELONGING TO THE

PARISH OF HAMPTON,

IN THE

COUNTY OF MIDDLESEX.

LONDON:

PRINTED BY G. KENT, NO. 1, STRAND LANE, STRAND.

1816.

Fig. 5. The cover of the list of local charities produced by William Jackson, the Vestry Clerk, in 1816

Fig. 6. The Rev. Prebendary Digby Ram, Vicar of Hampton 1882-1911

Fig. 7. Sir Frederick and Lady Dixon-Hartland; he was member of Parliament for the Uxbridge Division which included Hampton, from 1885 to 1909

Fig. 8. Jessamine House, drawn by Mrs D.E. Ablewhite from photographs

Fig. 9. Sketch Map of Hampton in 1800, drawn by A. Beckles-Willson

Key:

1. Chalk Farm
2. Workhouse
3. Farm
4. Manor House
5. *Maidenhead*
6. *White Horse*
7. Mrs Gouldsmith
8. Brick House
9. Dr Griffinhoofe
10. Mr Jackson's
11. *White Hart*
12. Dr Hemming
13. Site of house of John Blow
14. Mrs Hare
15. Castle House
16. *Black Horse*
17. *Worlds End*
18. Parish Houses
19. Hill House
20. Mrs Beard
21. Spring Grove – Mrs Greg
22. *Old Tavern*
23. *The Lamb*
24. Riverdale
25. *Red Lion*
26. Jessamine House
27. *Crown*
28. *Jolly Coopers*
29. *Bell*
30. *Feathers*
31. Chapel
32. St Mary's Church
33. Mrs Glover
34. Mrs Ancell
35. Miss Berryman
36. Mrs Garrick
37. Mrs Emma Jones
38. Duke of St Albans

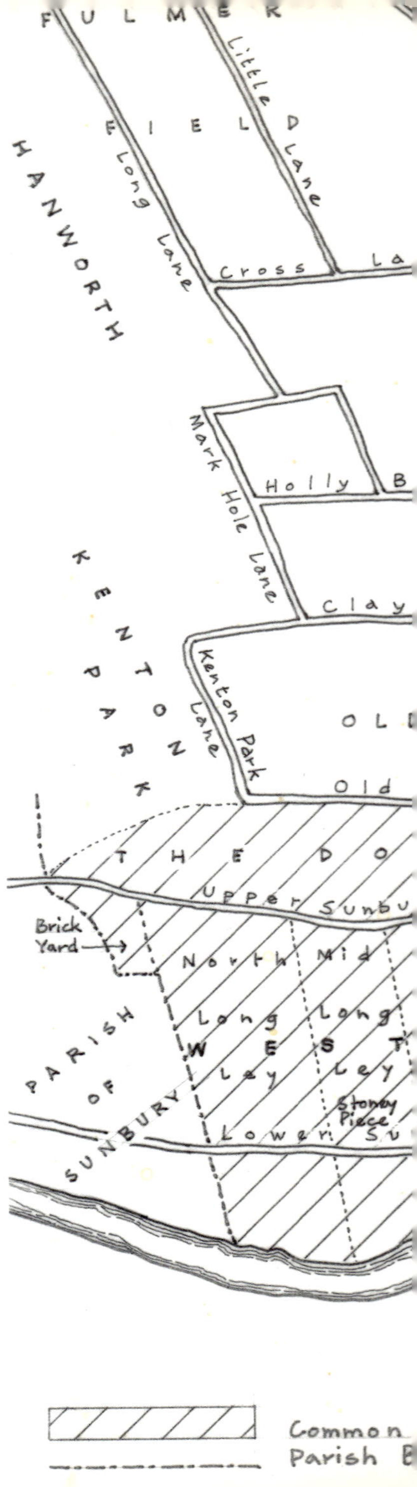

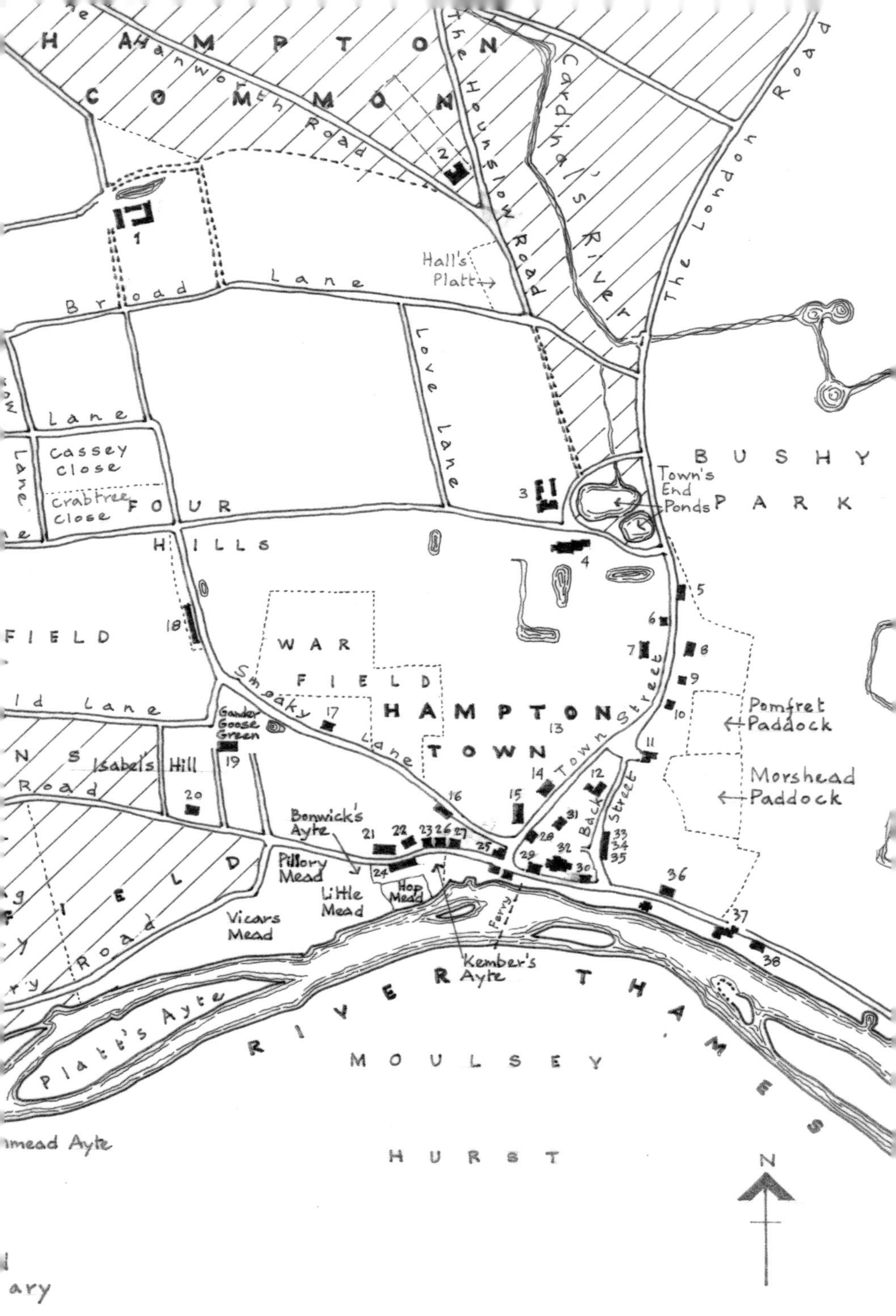
HAMPTON COMMON
Hanworth Road
The Hounslow Road
Cardinal's River
The London Road
Hall's Platt
Broad Lane
Love Lane
Lane
Cassey close
Crabtree close
FOUR HILLS
FIELD
BUSHY PARK
Town's End Ponds
WAR FIELD
HAMPTON TOWN
Town Street
Back Street
Smoaky Lane
Gander Goose Green
Isabel's Hill
Road
Pomfret Paddock
Morshead Paddock
Bonwick's Ayte
Pillory Mead
Little Mead
Hop Mead
Vicars Mead
Ferry
Kember's Ayte
Platt's Ayte
RIVER THAMES
MOULSEY
HURST
mead Ayte
N
1
2
3
4
5
6
7
8
9
10
11
12
13
14
15
16
17
18
19
20
21
22
23
24
25
26
27
28
29
30
31
32
33
34
35
36
37
38

Fig. 10. Castle House, drawn by Mrs D.E. Ablewhite from photographs

Fig. 11. The Waterworks c. 1880

Fig. 12. Headquarters of a Regatta on Garrick's Lawn

Fig. 13. Red Lion Square 1875

Fig. 14. Thames Street looking east towards St Mary's Church and the Bell Hotel

Fig. 15. The Old Grammar School

Fig. 16. Hill House, used as a school c. 1837-1854

Fig. 17. The Hampton Volunteer Fire Brigade established by Fire Brigade Captain Robert Graham

Fig. 18. The Fire Brigade in action at the fire which destroyed the old Red Lion in 1908

The English School

With the appointment of the Revd G. F. Heather to the Grammar School in 1868 and the success achieved by Mr Francis in building up the English School, the gap between the two grew wider. The introduction of a degree of compulsory education under Forster's Act of 1871 caused a further increase in the size of the English School and it is difficult to see how the building was able to accommodate both schools in the 1870s. Mr Francis retired in 1874 and was followed by Mr Henry Ripley, who achieved local distinction as organist and choirmaster and author of Hampton's first published history. The removal of the Grammar School in 1880 gave Mr Ripley a little more scope for teaching and he introduced an upper class to prepare boys for entry into commerce. By now there were 180 boys in the school. There was much rejoicing in 1891 when a Government grant made it no longer necessary to charge the hated weekly fee of 3d.

For years after the death of his wife Mr Ripley suffered from severe depression and in July 1902 he resigned; and a fortnight later committed suicide. His successor, Mr W. A. Cooke, had to cope with ever increasing numbers and the provision of new buildings became essential. This was helped by the passing of the Education Act of 1902 vesting authority in the County Councils. The first move had to be the provision of some overflow accommodation in the building which had housed the Navvies' Mission in Station Road until the completion of Percy Road School in 1907. In the course of time the old English School building was altered to make it suitable for use as a Parish Hall and it was used as such until the present hall was built.

The School of Industry and Station Road School

There was no attempt to provide free education for girls in Hampton until 1803 when a fund was raised to build a School of Industry. The Manor Court granted a small plot of land adjoining Bushy Park and the school opened in 1805 for the teaching of reading, writing and needlework, mainly to fit them for entry into service. The School of

Industry served its purpose and also served as a Sunday School until it was condemned as not meeting the requirements of the Education Act of 1871, and the parish was required to provide a new school. The opposition to the founding of a secular school was very vigorous and it was to prevent this that the Vicar of St James, Hampton Hill, the Revd F. J. Fitzwygram, provided a site in Station Road for the building of a girls' school on Anglican lines. This school served as the girls' school for Hampton until 1907, when the older girls moved to Percy Road School and Station Road School became the Infants' School. This school was closed in 1970, when a new school was built in Ripley Road, and the site was sold for the building of a block of maisonettes, Rushbury Court.

With the closure of the School of Industry in 1874 the building became firstly a Working Men's Club, then for a short time a Conservative Working Men's Club. From 1896 to 1912 it served as the Drill Hall of the Hampton Company of the Second Volunteer Battalion of the Middlesex Regiment. Then for a number of years it was in use as a petrol station and garage. The old building was demolished a few years ago and a new style petrol station built in its place. All that remains of the old School of Industry is the lintel stone commemorating its foundation in 1805.

Private Schools

Mr Jackson's School

There was no dearth of private schools in Hampton in the nineteenth century. There exists still an account book starting in 1787 for schools run by Mr Jackson for boys and by Mrs Ancell for girls. As this book covered 12 years or more and has several "brought forward from old book" entries, it is possible that both schools were in being in the 1770s.

John Jackson was the father of William Jackson, who was solicitor and parish clerk in Hampton for many years and father-in-law of

Mr F. J. Kent, who succeeded him, and who with his son, F. J. Kent and two succeeding generations carried on the firm of solicitors for more than a century. John Jackson was living at the house now known as The Hollies at the time of his death in 1814 and it is likely that he carried on his school there. It is possible that his son, William, carried on the school for a time for he was one of the candidates for the Mastership of the Grammar School in 1803. The account book shows that Mr Jackson also went to the Manor House as tutor to the children of Sir John Morshead and his wife Elizabeth (nee Frederick). In 1785 Mr Jackson had 85 pupils, a number being boarders with homes in London. Charges included slates, copy books, spelling books, pens and ink, firing, and the coach fare back home at the end of term. Tuition appears to have been 6d a week or, in some instances 7s. 6d. or 10s. 6d. a quarter, possibly depending on age. Books included Dilworth's Arithmetic Assistant and occasionally French and German textbooks, and a book entitles "The Cobweb to catch Flies".

Mrs Ancell's School

Mrs Ancell came to live at what is now Orme House in 1770 and it is possible that she started the school shortly afterwards. The account book for this school covers the years 1788 to 1805. The school was mainly for girls, of whom there were 12 in 1788, and small boys, of whom there were 6 in 1788. The charges shown in the account book are similar to those for Mr Jackson's school, but there was greater expenditure on French books. At least two of the pupils in 1788, Jenny and Patty Lawrence, became schoolmistresses in Hampton. Mrs Ancell died in 1799 and the school was taken over by Miss Truelove, who was joined by Miss Mence in 1802. The school closed in 1807 when Thomas Holloway who engraved the Raphael Cartoons, came to live at the house, which remained in private occupation until ca. 1849, when it was re-opened as a school by James Brooks and Charlotte his wife. The school later became associated with the school next door (see below) and at the time of the 1861 census was housing fourteen boarders. Orme House ceased to be connected with the school in about 1874 and reverted to private use.

The School of Miss Berryman and Mrs Francis (later the Misses Lawrence)

The school at the Old Grange had the longest existence of any of the private schools in Hampton. It was certainly in being in 1803, when the account book referred to above shows that a pupil of Miss Truelove and Miss Mence moved to Miss Berryman's school. Louisa Berryman was joined by Miss Patty Lawrence, who married William Francis, a music teacher, and they ran the school together until Miss Berryman's death in 1842. Mrs Patty Francis then carried on until her death at the age of 84 in 1863. At the time of the 1841 census Mrs Francis's nieces Jane and Louisa Lawrence were on the staff and there were 15 girls boarding. In 1851 there were 16 boarders including Mrs Francis's greatnieces Elizabeth and Louisa. Mrs Francis was succeeded by her nieces Sarah and Jane and later by her great-nieces, who kept the Old Grange school in being until 1910 when, with their lack of qualifications and the greater control of education, they found it expedient to close. Nevertheless the school had plenty of scholastic successes and it provided all that was required for young ladies who were going to stay at home until they married or to look after their parents if they did not marry.

Alfred House School

The Revd William Church came to live at Alfred House (now Park and Barham Houses) in ca. 1812 and ran a gentlemen's boarding academy there for a number of years, probably until his death in 1829. In 1814 he stood against the Revd Samuel Hemming for the curacy and was elected by a small majority. Mrs Jenny Berryman who, as Jenny Lawrence, had attended Mrs Ancell's school, was his assistant and carried on the school until about 1844. At the time of the 1841 census she had two governesses and there were 15 boarders.

Hill House School

Mr J. E. Mills, a former Naval officer, lived firstly at what is now the Hampton Clinic in Station Road. It is not known whether he started his school there, but about 1837 he acquired the tenancy of Hill House (demolished in 1902 to make way for the Station Road filter beds) and converted it into a school. Hill House was mainly a commercial and practical school and its most distinguished pupil, from 1842 to 1845, was Field Marshal Lord Roberts. At about this time there were 16 boarders in the school, which was run by Mr Mills with aid of a governess. By the 1851 census Mr Mills, then already aged 67, had ten boarders. He appears to have retired about 1854, when the school closed.

Mr Walton's Academy

Mr William Walton came to Hampton about 1824. He was a candidate for the Mastership of the Grammar School on the death of the Revd Dr Hemming in 1828, but no appointment was made and Mr Walton started a school of his own in the house formerly occupied by Dr Hemming between Church Street and High Street. The school catered for boys whose parents were serving their country abroad and was run on classical lines. It was said that instruction was based on "the energetic flogging of pupils and copious dosing of them with brimstone and treacle". Mr Walton's most distinguished pupil was the first Marquis of Dufferin and Ava, later Viceroy of India. A number of his other pupils achieved distinction in various ways, one, Evan McGregor, becoming Permanent Secretary of the Admiralty. In 1851 there were 30 boarders aged between 9 and 15, as well as Mr Walton's four sons. One of his sons built the railway bridge at Benares, which was opened by the Marquis of Dufferin when Viceroy and was named Dufferin Bridge. Mr Walton retired about 1870, but lived on at the house, where the school was carried on for a few more years.

Mr Hammond's Commercial School

Mr William Hammond started his Commercial School at what is now Penn's Place in 1862. The wide curriculum included the Classics, Arithmetic, Bookkeeping, Mensuration and Land Surveying, Algebra, Trigonometry, French, English, History, Geography,

Chemistry and Physics. The school was affiliated to the Art and Science Department of the Committee of the Council on Education and appears to have had considerable success in examinations. For a number of years it was large enough to have two cricket teams. Mr Hammond, who was also Secretary of the Hampton Court Gas Co. and holder of many parish offices, died in 1892 and the school was kept on by his daughters as a boys' preparatory school for a few more years.

Pembroke House School

In 1888 Mr J. F. Ellis, who had been an assistant master at the Grammar School, started a boys' preparatory school in Broad Lane, Pembroke House School. On the opposite side of the road was a playing field, now the site of Linden House. The curriculum was designed to prepare boys for entrance into public schools and the Army and Navy. The school flourished for more than 70 years and was closed in 1966 to allow demolition and the building of new houses in Broad Lane and Albury Close.

CHURCH AND CHAPEL

St Mary's Church

In 1798 the Hon and Revd Gerald Valerian Wellesley, younger brother of the Marquis of Wellesley and the Duke of Wellington, was appointed Vicar of Hampton. Hampton had seen little of its previous vicar, the Revd Abraham Blackborne, who was a pluralist, but the Hon G. V. Wellesley was also Chaplain of the Chapel Royal at Hampton Court where his mother, the Countess of Mornington, had apartments and he took a greater part in parish life than either his predecessor or his successor, the Revd S. J. Goodenough. Fortunately Hampton had three able resident ministers at this time, the Revd Dr Thomas Morgan (1800 – 1814), The Revd William Church (1814 – 1823) and the Revd John Merewether (1823 – 1832)

Exactly when the old St Mary's church was built is not known, but the tower had to be rebuilt in 1679 and in 1726 the church was enlarged by building an aisle on the north side, as well as a schoolroom which also served as a Vestry meeting place. In view of the increase in the population in the early part of the nineteenth century the Vestry decided on 9 July 1821 that a further enlargement was essential. A committee with the Revd William Church as chairman was set up and Mr Thomas Hardwick, one of Sir Christopher Wren's successors as Surveyor General of Works, offered his services free, putting forward three alternative proposals. The plan approved by the committee involved taking down the schoolroom, the robing room, and the north wall of the chancel – a plan which would require the building of a new school and vestry room.

When it came to the question of raising the money it seemed opportune to seek the aid of King George IV, for not only was he Patron of the Advowson of the Vicarage and Lord of the Manor of Hampton Court, but his forebears had contributed liberally to the building of the tower in 1679 and of the north aisle in 1726. Eventually the Crown agreed to contribute as long as seats were provided for the occupants of Crown property at Hampton Court. Secondly an appeal was made to the Society for the Enlargement and Building of Churches, but this body would only contribute if more than half the additional seating was to be free. Thirdly, it was confidently expected that voluntary contributions would be forthcoming from those whose station in life would enable them to do so. By 1824 it was concluded that the funds which could be raised would be inadequate and the proposal to enlarge the church was deferred.

In April 1826 the question was re-opened and the Archdeacon of Middlesex, George Owen Cambridge, was asked to intercede with the Bishop of London. In a letter to the curate of St. Mary's, the Revd John Merewether, Archdeacon Cambridge deplored the lack of accommodation for the increasing population and "lamented, as every reflecting person must do, the spiritual wants of the Poor and the consequent Immorality and Profligacy which must prevail in so important and respectable a parish as Hampton." A new committee was formed under the Revd John Merewether and for the first time the possibility of entirely rebuilding the church was mentioned. The committee decided against this, however, and advertised in The Times and the Morning Chronicle for the submission of plans for the enlargement of the church. Meanwhile the church surveyor, Mr Henry Walker of Hampton Wick, reported that the state of the walls was such that they would not support a new roof. Later Mr Edward Lapidge, of Hampton Wick, reported very unfavourably on the state of the tower, which he found to have scarcely any footings, and concluded that it would need to be rebuilt, a conclusion which was soon to be reinforced by an Act of God in the form of a stroke of lightning.

Twelve plans were submitted in response to the advertisement. Of these the one submitted by Mr Edward Lapidge was chosen by the committee with certain amendments. A new approach was made to the Treasury, resulting in an offer to meet one third of the cost up to a limit of £1666 13s. 4d., provided that the remaining two thirds could be raised by voluntary subscription. The financial position was then helped considerably by the agreement of H.M's Commissioners for the Building of New Churches to grant £3000 for the building of a new chapel at Hampton Wick, whereupon the Society for Building and Enlarging Churches agreed to transfer to St Mary's a grant of £500 already made for a chapel at Hampton Wick. With the improved prospects of national support it was decided to make a new appeal to parishioners and a total of £1233 13s. was promised, but when it came to the point of giving the sum fell short by £695 and it was decided to return the contributions already made.

The choice of Mr Lapidge's plan was endorsed by the parish in vestry assembled on 30 July 1827; authority was given for the raising of a loan of £2500 on the security of the parish rates; and a new church building committee was formed. Apart from the bare cost of rebuilding the church there were a number of other expenses – the facing of the church with Suffolk bricks, the building of an extra vault, the provision of new stone steps at the entrance and of iron railings and a gate, the provision of a flagpole and of a heating system. Then there would be the cost of removing and re-erecting the monuments, the replacement of the clock and the purchase and hanging of a new set of bells. The Crown's contribution was raised to £2000, but it was still necessary to raise a loan of £5500.

The lowest tender submitted, that of Mr Charles Smith of Peternoster Row for £6355, was accepted. Arrangements were made for the sale by auction of the materials of the old church by Messrs Fricker of Kingston and for the use of the Great Hall of Hampton Court Palace for the holding of services while the building was taking place. Vestry meetings during this period were held at the Red Lion and the Bell. At a Vestry meeting held on 18 November 1829 the Duke of Clarence and the Bishop of London were thanked for their assistance in obtaining the use of the Great Hall and the Revd Mr Merewether was thanked for his care and attention in bringing about the rebuilding of the church. The Duke of Clarence was present and signed the minutes of the meeting.

The old church was closed after evening service on 27 December 1829 and the materials were sold on 6 January 1830. Mr Fricker, however, failed to hand over the proceeds of the sale until several months later when threatened with the law. Demolition started on 27 January. The Duke of Clarence laid the foundation stone on 15 April 1830 with a silver gilt trowel and, following the usual custom, a set of coins of the realm was placed inside the stone. Each workman was given 2s. 6d. and flannel waistcoats were presented to the Clerk of Works and the two foremen.

The consecration of the new church took place on 1 September 1831. A man was posted on the far bank of the river to signal the approach of the Royal party, which consisted of Queen Adelaide, Prince George of Cambridge, and his sister Augusta. The roads were blocked with carriages a quarter of a mile away from the church and eighteen officers of the newly formed Metropolitan Police were present to keep order; and so, more than ten years after the decision of the Vestry, the larger church of St Mary became a reality. But this was not the end of the Church Building Committee's problems, for little more than two years later the safety of the tower was endangered by the loosening of the bell frame and the ringing of the bells had to be suspended until the frame had been strengthened by iron braces and bolts.

St Mary's Church struck a bad patch in 1844, when the Revd Edward Johnstone was appointed vicar in succession to the Revd S. J. Goodenough. There are good grounds for the view that Mr Johnstone was a cantankerous man who was frequently in dispute with his parishioners. The failure of the Literary Society largely because of his truculence has been noted, and some of the vitupera-tive letters he wrote to the Commissioners of Woods and Forests about the rectorial tithes are still in existence. At the Easter Vestry of 1859 the churchwardens refused to sit next to him.

In February 1859 the Surrey Comet reported that "various unpleasant rumours reflecting upon the moral conduct and demeanour of the Vicar are prevalent in Hampton". The church-wardens felt it their duty to report the position to the Archdeacon who, however, regarded the charges as no more than idle rumour. Not satisfied with this, the inhabitants called a public meeting and a committee was appointed to act as a deputation to the Bishop, but he too refused to take any action. Meanwhile intense hostility was shown to the Vicar whenever he made an appearance and on two occasions he caused inhabitants to be summoned for assaulting him. On one of these the people expressed their opinion by making a presentation to one of the defendants at a public meeting to cover his fine and expenses. Matters came to a head in June 1860 when a case was brought against Mr Johnstone in the Queen's Bench for indecently assaulting a parishioner's wife, but the jury could not agree and Mr Johnstone was discharged. He disappeared for a time, but nothing could now ease the relationship between the Vicar and his flock and arrangements were made for an exchange of livings between him and the Revd James Burrow of Warehorne in Kent. With a hundred years gone by one wonders whether Mr Johnstone was the victim of a vendetta against him by parishioners who were understandably offended by his truculent behaviour and were determined upon revenge. It would be charitable to end this chapter of St Mary's history by noting that his ecclesiastical superiors believed him innocent and that after what was presumably a fair trial he was given the benefit of a doubt.

Contemporary newspaper accounts show that the Revd James Burrow, if not cantankerous in the Johnstone manner, was of a disputatious nature and came into conflict with his parishioners on more than one occasion, particularly in his secular capacity as chairman of the Vestry. He made himself unpopular over the 1866 Grammar School plan by his acceptance of the Charity Commissioners' proposals when the Vestry held that his duty was to be neutral. He strongly objected to the reporting of Vestry meetings by the local press. On one occasion, when the Vestry was discussing pollution of well water by sewage Mr Burrow said that he knew as much about water analysis as anybody and that he was satisfied that the water was good for drinking. The complainants, however, brought in a professor of chemistry, who was also an FRS, who reported "It is altogether a nasty water and in my opinion quite unfit for family use." On the other hand Ripley wrote of Mr Burrow as the kindest hearted of men.

The Revd Mr Burrow became partially paralysed towards the end of 1881 and in January 1882 was snow-bound in a train for several hours. It was considered that this experience contributed to his sudden death in June 1882. After a delay of several months the Revd Digby Ram, Vicar of Teddington, was appointed to succeed him. Mr Ram found the old vicarage unfit to live in and rented Grove House until the new vicarage was completed in 1884. Mr Ram introduced a number of innovations, including the singing of carols from the church tower on New Year's Eve and the institution of a Parish Tea. Another innovation, which was presumably not made without good reason, was the awarding of prizes to boys for good behaviour in church.

The churchyard was closed in 1883 and a new cemetery was opened in Holly Bush Lane. Several alterations were made to the church in 1884, including the installation of new pews, and in 1887, to mark Queen Victoria's Golden Jubilee, a chancel was built. In 1898 the organ was rebuilt.

It cannot be doubted that the Revd Digby Ram was the outstanding vicar of the 19th century and that he was greatly liked and respected by the parish. In 1907, when he announced for a second time his firm intention of resigning, a public meeting was held at the new Percy Road School and 400 inhabitants unanimously agreed to the sending of a letter to the Bishop of Kensington asking that Mr Ram should remain at Hampton, which he did until the end of 1911.

Digby Ram's views about the re-marriage of divorced persons in church were strong and orthodox at the time and it came as no surprise that when, in April 1900, Maud Chester, the granddaughter of Mrs Grove of Garrick Villa, and her future husband, who had been divorced, were granted a licence to marry in St Mary's Church, Digby Ram and his curate not only refused to take the service, but forbade the use of the organ, bells or choir, and ordered the return to Garrick Villa of flowers that had been sent to the church. As the ceremony was being performed by a priest from St David's cathedral and the Vicar of Borrowdale, a commotion was caused when a member of the congregation claimed that there was "just cause and impediment" and that the wedding should not take place. After an exchange of words the officiating clergy continued with the wedding. The objector continued his protest by writing several times to the Bishop of London, but his letters were not acknowledged. Digby Ram also took a strong line against the Act of 1905 allowing marriage to a deceased wife's sister and announced his refusal to officiate at such a ceremony.

The Church of St Theodore

The first move towards the establishment of a Roman Catholic church in Hampton came in July 1897, when Mr Michael Farmer, the proprietor of the Copying Apparatus Co., was granted permission for the celebration of Mass at his house, St Winifred's in Belgrade Road. Mr Farmer's second son, Sir Mark Farmer, achieved distinction when he was appointed surgeon dentist to King George V. Thirty years passed before the Church of St Theodore was dedicated.

The Independent Chapel

The first dissenting chapel in Hampton was established by the Congregationalists in 1810 on a small piece of ground 24 feet by 30 feet with a right of way from High Street. The land formed part of a malthouse which had been in use for at least a hundred years. The chapel was in regular use until 1870, when a new Congregational Church was built in High Street, Hampton Hill. The old chapel was sold by auction and converted into two houses, known as Chapel Cottages. The building still exists and is now used by a printing firm.

The Wesleyan Chapel

The Wesleyan Chapel in Church Street was founded in 1861. An early picture shows that it then had a tower on the west side. The chapel remained in use until the building of the Methodist Church in Percy Road in 1925, after which it was unused for many years. Recently it has been in use by manufacturers of electrical equipment.

Mission Halls

The latter part of the nineteenth century was a great time for revivalist missions, of which Hampton had two. One of these was founded by Mrs J. P. Kitchin in the grounds of the Manor House, known as the Chalet Mission Hall, which was also the meeting place of the Band of Hope. The Chalet Mission thrived for nearly twenty years with congregations of well over a hundred, but the death of Mr J. P. Kitchin in 1901 brought it to an end.

In 1890 the London City Mission was running revivalist meetings in a tent in Milton Road. In December 1892, with help from the Kitchin family, a brick mission hall was built. The Milton Road Mission faded away in the 1920s and the building was acquired by All Saints' Church as a meeting hall and used until the new hall beside the church was opened, after which the old mission hall became a confectioner's depot.

With the great influx of men engaged on the extensions to the water works in 1893 a Navvies' Mission was set up in temporary quarters in the Upper Sunbury Road at the instigation of the Revd Digby Ram. The building also served as a reading room and club. Before long the building was taken down and re-erected in Station Road. Owing to lack of support it was closed in July 1895. A new one was started in December 1897, but did not last for long. The corrugated iron building was used as a temporary school while Percy Road School was being built. It was later removed to the corner of Oldfield and Percy Roads, where it was used as a club for employees of the Metropolitan Water Board until the Ashley Road premises were built, and is still in use by an engineering company.

COMMUNICATIONS

Road

Before 1800 there were stage coach services between Ludgate Hill, Holborn, the Old Bailey, Fleet Street and Hampton. The number of coaches increased gradually and by 1823 there was also a service from the Bell to London and back. By 1840 there was an omnibus service from the Bell five times a day and the London to Sunbury coaches also called at the Bell six times a day in each direction. There were also cart and waggon services for goods, and

Hampton had its own long established firm of carriers, the Wooldridge family. Coach and omnibus services continued to improve and by 1860 the Richmond Conveyance Company was running an omnibus service between St Paul's Churchyard and Chertsey, calling at Hampton, every twenty minutes from 9 a.m. to 9 p.m., but the railway was almost in sight and the live horse could not compete with the iron horse. There was, nevertheless, still a place for the horse omnibus for some local journeys. From 1883 onwards a two-horse omnibus provided a service between Hanworth Edge and Fulwell Station and from 1888 Mr Brett's omnibus ran six times a day from the Red Lion to Kingston and back with an extra trip on Saturday evenings until the start of the new century when the electric tramway displaced it.

It was just before the end of the century, in July 1899, that the Middlesex County Council consented to a proposal by the London United Tramway Company to lay down a network of tracks in south-west Middlesex, in particular one from Isleworth to Hampton Court via Twickenham and Hampton. To bring the scheme to fruition it was necessary to widen the road most of the way from Hampton Hill to Hampton Court. Property had to be acquired and a number of houses had to be demolished, including the William IV public house and two shops at the corner of Church Street and Hampton Court Road. Garrick's Villa was bought for demolition and the fence of Bushy Park was set back, despite Parliamentary opposition. In the end Garrick's Villa was saved because the General Manager of the company, Mr (later Sir) Clifton Robinson, took a fancy to it and had a siding made in the wall to take his private tram. The first tram ran through to Hampton Court in May 1903. It is said that Sir Clifton Robinson was once asked about the provision of shelters for those waiting for trams and his reply was that there would be no need as the passengers would do their waiting in the tram. This was doubtless a fair reply because the trams used then to run at intervals of about a minute. This popular tram service ran until 1929, when it was replaced by a trolley-bus service (No. 667) and this in turn was replaced by the present bus service (No. 267), which follows the same route, but is less frequent than Sir Clifton Robinson's trams.

The Railway

Hampton's first contact with the railway was in 1840 when a coach service provided a connection with the Southampton line at Ditton Marsh station. In 1849 the line to Hampton Court started, but both these stations were some way away from Hampton and a meeting was held at the Red Lion in January 1862 to canvass support for a Metropolitan and Thames Valley Railway with a station at Hampton. The meeting was unanimous in its support and the necessary Bill was rushed through Parliament at great speed.

The original plan for the Thames Valley Railway was for the line to pass to the south of Kempton Park between Hampton and Sunbury, but in the end it made a detour to the north of the park. Construction of the line proceeded rapidly and the first down train left Waterloo at 7.35 a.m. on 1 November 1864; five minutes later the first up train left Shepperton. The fares from Waterloo to Shepperton were 3s first class, 2s. 4d. second class, and 1s. 7d. third class and the journey took one hour. In 1894 a third line was built at Shacklegate junction to connect Hampton and Kingston.

At Hampton station there was only one entrance, on the down side, and passengers had to cross the line to the up platform until 1897, when a new road (Ashley Road) and entrance to the station were made on the north side.

After the first enthusiasm had worn off there were complaints about the service; the last train from Waterloo left at 10.40 p.m. (1876); no foot-warmers or mats were provided for second class passengers (1879); trains were slow and infrequent (1887); third class seasons were not obtainable (1889); trains often ran five or ten minutes late (1890) though the journey from Hampton to Waterloo was scheduled to take 33 minutes.

Two other proposals for railways serving Hampton did not materialize. In 1881 plans were put forward for an Esher, Hounslow and Southall Railway. This would have crossed the Thames at Hampton and run parallel to the eastern boundary of Kempton Park and under the Thames Valley line. There was to be a station near Oldfield Road and another at Hanworth. A meeting to support the proposal was held, but was attended by only seven people. In 1885 the Hampton Ratepayers' Association proposed an extension to Hampton of the Underground line to Hounslow, but this found little support.

River

At the turn of the eighteenth century boats could be hired to carry passengers between London and Hampton, but the river was mainly used by barges carrying merchandise of all sorts. Navigation at that time was hazardous because, with no control of the flow, flooding, strong currents and uncharted shoals could be met in winter, while in summer the river could be so shallow as to be impassable for barges. From 1775 tolls were levied by the City of London for the improvement of the river up to the boundary of its jurisdiction at Staines. The arrival of the City Barge carrying the Navigation Committee on an inspection of the river was a noteworthy event in Hampton. The excitement of the occasion is vividly portrayed in a water colour painting by Rowlandson in the possession of the Borough of Kingston upon Thames.

With the income from the tolls great improvements were made in the early part of the century. A chain of locks was constructed, the one at Molesey being completed in 1815, and for the rest of the century the Thames was at its zenith as a trading route. The new church clock was brought to Hampton by river in 1809 and most of the materials for the new church in 1830. In 1855 barges started to bring the coal required by the new Water Companies and this has been the most important commodity in Hampton's river traffic ever since.

Post, Telegraph and Telephone

In the 1820s, if not before, letters were despatched to London at 7.30 a.m. and 3 p.m. and arrived from London at the Thames Street Post Office at 9 a.m. and 1 p.m. By 1840, the year of the introduction of the penny post , there were three deliveries a day in Hampton, made by two postmen. In 1888, in response to complaints the GPO undertook to deliver letters to London the same afternoon if posted before mid-day so that they could be answered and the replies received in Hampton the following morning. There were then four deliveries a day, but only one on Sunday. The withdrawal of the Sunday delivery in 1892 caused so much indignation that the service was very soon restored.

In October 1870 telegraph poles started to appear in Hampton and in August 1872 the Vestry agreed to allow the erection of poles along the Upper Sunbury Road so that Sunbury could benefit from the new invention.

The coming of the telephone service was delayed by a County Council decree in 1891 that all telephone wires were to be laid underground. After ten years had passed the Urban District Council appreciated the need for telephone communication between its offices and the fire stations at Hampton and Hampton Hill, the sewage works and the Isolation Hospital, and when given no option agreed to the erection of poles, the only outstanding question being whether they should be wooden or ornamental iron ones, the vote in the end being for wooden ones.

THE GROWTH OF HAMPTON

The census figure for 1801 gave Hampton a population of 1722, including a few who were living in what is now Hampton Hill. By 1861 the population of Hampton proper was 1903, not a very rapid rate of growth, but with the coming of the railway and the rapidly increasing population generally it went up to 3449 in 1891 and 4222 in 1901.

The Tangley Park (Marling Park) Estate

Mr Grover, of Tangley Park Farm (formerly Chalk Farm), was the first to provide country homes for London business men travelling to and fro each day. Before the end of 1863 he was advertising plots of land for sale. To keep up the quality of the area he intended that each house should be set in from one to four acres of garden. So sure was he of the rapid development of the area that he built a hotel, the Royal Hotel, in 1867 near the eastern end of Hanworth Road. It was never used as such and in 1869 it was bought by the Female Orphan Home, which had been founded at Walthamstow in 1855. The home provided a worthy outlet for Hampton's charitable instincts until its closure in 1936, followed shortly by demolition, except for the hall now used by The Brethren. Mr Grover's housing scheme was no more successful than his hotel and he sold the farm as a going concern to Mr A. Stanford, who continued the attempt to develop it, but eventually gave up and sold it to the Estate Investment and Villa Farm Company in 1883. The company tried by various means to dispose of it as "choice sites for medium class residences with extensive gardens". A new road was made (later known as Percy Road and The Avenue) to link the estate with the railway station, but after seven years only a few houses had been built, including one ("Broadmead") for the secretary and one ("Chesterfield") for the surveyor; some of the land became nurseries. By August 1889 the company was in difficulties and in 1890 had to go into liquidation, paying out £1 for each £10 share.

The estate was then bought by members of the Marling Family and the name was changed to the Marling Park Estate. The building of houses proceeded gradually, but the greater part found use as nursery land which, now (1973) mostly derelict, awaits the housing development planned for it 110 years ago.

The Buckingham Estate

It is difficult to see why the area near the apex formed by Buckingham Road and Hanworth Road developed more rapidly than Tangley Park, it being the part of Hampton furthest away from a railway station. By 1883, however, a new community had been formed there with a bus service to Fulwell Station. Ripley, writing in 1884, deplored these developments. "Property in Hampton is not what it was; London is gradually drawing nigher and nigher; the building interests have fixed their covetous eyes upon its pleasant meads and shady lanes; the air is rife with rumours of plots and plans for the improvement away of its peaceful and primitive rusticity; and soon in all human probability the votaries of hod and trowel will carry the neighbourhood by storm . . . "

The River Hill Estate

The River Hill Estate was formerly the garden and orchard of Spring Grove. Major Francis Tipping Ball bought this land in 1876 and in 1878 laid it out in building plots, naming the roads Plevna, Varna and Belgrade, possibly because it was the time of the Russo-Turkish war, when these towns were news. He stipulated that the houses were to cost not less than £250 and that, apart from a few plots fronting on New Street (Station Road) and intended for use as shops, there was to be no building for trade or manufacture and no public house or place for the sale of beer or spirits. In the event Varna Road was not extended to join Belgrade Road as intended and a cabinet works was built there. Unlike the other nineteenth century housing developments in Hampton, the River Hill Estate was built to saturation in a few years.

Stain Hill Park

Stain Hill Park was another grandiose housing scheme which came to nought. The Ordnance Survey map of 1894-6 shows the lay-out of the roads, which were to be made up of large detached houses. A few of these had been built when the Southwark and

Vauxhall Water Company obtained approval for the construction of another reservoir and all that now remains between the Upper and Lower Sunbury Roads is the two pairs of semi-detached houses known as Kempton Villas and the roadway between them which formerly led into the estate.

The Wolsey (Humber) Estate

Mr Humber, the bicycle manufacturer, when he retired to Teddington in the 1890s, decided to occupy his leisure time by building houses. The Wolsey Estate included a number of detached houses in the rectangle formed by Percy Road, Priory Road, and the new Chestnut Avenue, and also two pairs of semi-detached houses in Priory Road. Miss Humber lived in the detached house at the corner of Priory Road and Chestnut Avenue for many years.

The Manor House Estate

What was later to become Hampton's biggest development started in 1897 with the decision of the Earl of Carlisle to break up the Manor House Estate. At an auction sale at the Bell on 27 October only about a dozen lots were disposed of, out of the 125 lots offered, but many more were sold afterwards by private treaty and so began the spread of housing to the south side of Broad Lane, Wensleydale Road, Barlow Road and Tudor Road early in the new century and then to Ormond Avenue.

LOCAL GOVERNMENT – THE LOCAL BOARD AND THE URBAN DISTRICT COUNCIL

An important stage in the evolution of local government took place in 1858 with the passing of an Act which allowed "places having a known or defined boundary" to elect Local Boards, which were to have wider powers than the Vestry. Moreover, Local Boards could raise loans for important enterprises whereas the Vestry had to rely on personal loans. Local Boards were authorized to deal, amongst other things, with drainage and sewage disposal, road maintenance, water supply, the suppression of nuisances, building plans and the provision of watching and lighting, and could act as Burial Boards. All that was required was a majority vote of the ratepayers in favour of adoption, but there was proper provision for appeal and the holding of an official inquiry.

The question whether Hampton should have a Local Board divided the village into two violently opposed factions and feeling ran very high. The events of those days are described in detail in Twickenham Local History Society publication No. 10. Briefly, at a meeting held on 9 March 1865 a motion to adopt the Local Board system was defeated on a show of hands by 39 votes to 27, at which there was tremendous cheering. A poll was demanded and both sides redoubled their activities. On the one hand an association of residents was formed under the chairmanship of Lord Charles Fitzroy to press for a Local Board. On the other hand a "No Local" committee was formed. The voting was firmly against having a Local Board, by 254 to 128, and government by Vestry and the parish officers continued. But with the passing of the Public Health Act of 1872 Hampton found itself willy-nilly under the Kingston Rural Sanitary Authority as far as health matters were concerned. This, as well as subservience to the Kingston Board of Guardians, was more than many Hamptonians could stomach and the attitude to Local Boards gradually changed so that by 1884 a small majority of ratepayers voted in favour. By this time the Local Government Board had lost patience with Hampton and turned down the request to form a Local Board, arguing that Hampton was too small a community to have one.

No progress was made until the Middlesex County Council came into being in 1888. At the request of a number of ratepayers an inquiry was held and in the course of time the County Council decided to make Hampton an Urban District with a Local Board of nine members. An election was held and the Local Board against which some Hamptonians had held out so long met for the first time on 7 August 1890. It had a stormy start for Mr Auguste de Wette, who was elected chairman, resigned after 3/4 hour in protest at the election of Mr F. A. Kent as Clerk, believing that Mr Kent had insufficient experience. Mr Sanders, of Hampton Hill, was then elected chairman, and an open competition was held for the office of Clerk. Mr Kent was chosen and so carried on what was in essence the appointment held by four generations before him. The Hampton Local Board was converted to an Urban District Council at the beginning of 1895 and the U.D.C. remained responsible for the local government of Hampton until its assimilation in the Borough of Twickenham in 1937.

The first meeting of the Board took place at Mr Kent's office at Castle House. Several possible sites for the Board's offices were considered and some rooms over Ashby's Bank (where Barclays Bank now is) at the corner of Station Road and High Street were chosen as temporary offices and a yard at what used to be Mr Walton's school was rented for storage. In 1894 the Board decided to move their offices to Park House, High Street, where they remained until 1902 when, in spite of many protests, Rose Hill was purchased to provide offices as well as the free library. On the amalgamation with Twickenham the offices were no longer needed, but the library remained.

The Fire Brigade

The first mention of the maintenance of a fire engine is in the Churchwardens' accounts in 1789, when an engine house was built. From then on a fire engine keeper was appointed at the Easter Vestry. A number of houses in Hampton still carry fire insurance marks. The inadequacy of Hampton's fire service was acutely felt in 1867 when a large part of Rose Villa (Beveree) was burnt down. Although the water works had been in operation for some twelve years it was still necessary on this occasion to send a messenger to Twickenham to get the mains charged, and when the water did come through, the hose was too short. In 1870 the engine keeper made a plea for a new engine, complaining that he was often insulted by people who called his engine the "water squirt". Three years later the Vestry voted to buy a steam fire engine, but the resolution was rescinded six months later.

It was not until 1885 that the Hampton Volunteer Brigade was formed under the captaincy of Mr R. G. Graham of St Albans. Entertainments were held over the next four months to raise the money for a new manual engine, and it happened that the day after it arrived it had to be used to put out a fire in Thames Street. Before long the brigade was answering calls from neighbouring areas. In 1886 they reached a fire at Richmond within half-an-hour of receiving the telegram.

Captain Graham rapidly built up a very efficient brigade which soon became the pride of the village. Before long they were taking part in and winning national competitions. Their efficiency was put to a severe test in the early hours of 28 March 1892 when the Bell caught fire. In all eleven brigades attended, but though there was no shortage of water, the manual engines could not provide sufficient power to use it effectively, thus emphasizing again the need for a steam fire engine. A steamer was eventually purchased and both this and the old manual engine were used until 1900 when a new steam fire engine of the latest design was bought.

The year 1897 was an eventful one for the brigade. The very latest type of three-ladder fire escape was brought into use and on 25 September the foundation stone of the long-awaited fire station was laid. The opening took place on Saturday afternoon, 19 February 1898 with a ceremonial removal of the fire escape and engine from the old shed behind the Bell to the new premises in Thames Street. Soon the Southwark and Vauxhall Water Co. had its own fire brigade and the two brigades worked in friendly rivalry for many years to come.

Allotments

One of the early actions of the Local Board was to give some practical aid to those in need by obtaining more land for use as allotments. Hampton's first allotments were part of the Vicar's glebe land in Percy Road, but this was insufficient to meet the demand and in 1893 the Board sought the lease of some land in Bushy Park. The Board of Works replied curtly that the land was required for the service of the Royal parks and could not be dispensed with. But in August 1893 Hampton's M.P., Sir Frederick Dixon-Hartland, asked in Parliament whether it was true that the request had been turned down and it was not long before the Chief Commissioner of Works found that, after all, a 13-acre field could be spared. By March 1894 the plots were marked out and are still in use.

The Sewage Disposal Works

In 1867 Parliament acknowledged that the pollution of the Thames by untreated sewage could no longer be tolerated and passed an Act forbidding the discharge of sewage into the river between Lechlade and Putney. The Act came into force in 1869 and posed an enormous problem for towns and villages in the Lower Thames Valley. Twenty-five schemes were put forward and were considered by the Lower Thames Valley Main Sewerage Board, but after years of frustration the Board gave up and it was left to the separate authorities to make their own arrangements. Hampton, having refused to form a Local Board, had no means of raising the necessary funds and in October 1867 formally adopted the cesspool system. After twenty years of this the parishioners began to demand the provision of an efficient disposal system and in 1886 a Parochial Committee was asked to devise one at a cost of £100. As the Vicar said at a Vestry meeting in 1887, the sewerage question had been hanging over them for some time like the sword of Damocles, and now the thread seemed very much like breaking. It was largely the question of sewage disposal which swayed opinion in favour of a Local Board and once the Local Board had been formed, it set about the question in earnest. Several sites for a disposal area were considered, including Bushy Park, and one was eventually chosen at the north-west corner of Hampton. The then novel bacteriological method of treatment was adopted and drains were laid across Bushy Park and Home Park to take the treated effluent to the Thames below the Water Gallery. The whole system, which cost £62,000, was brought into use by 14 October 1899, when it was formally declared open by Sir Frederick Dixon-Hartland. So successful did the system prove that sanitary engineers from all over Europe came to Hampton to see it in operation.

Roads

For years the state of Hampton's roads was a subject for complaint, especially after they had been excavated by the water companies. At times the roads were just muddy tracks, but at other times watering was necessary to lay the dust. In 1870 and again in 1880 the ratepayers banded together to try to force the parish officers to do something about them, though exactly what was not clear. In 1895 a trailer carrying a massive boiler sank up to the hubs in Thames Street, and a furniture van became stuck in the mud in Hanworth Road and had to be unloaded before it could be moved. By the end of the century, however, asphalting of the roads had started. At about this time the Highways Committee started to change the names of the roads. The main changes were that part of New Street became Station Road and the other part Tudor Road; Clay Lane became Priory Road; Hanworth Long Lane became Oak Avenue; and Wolsey Gardens became Chestnut Avenue.

PEOPLE AND HOUSES

Few Hampton residents of the nineteenth century became national figures. From about 1820 onwards most of the larger houses were occupied by merchants, lawyers, civil servants, retired Army and

Naval Officers, and a few who had the means to enable them to live the life of a country gentleman. Space will permit the mention of only a few of these; many others were noteworthy for their devotion to the well-being of Hampton.

The Manor House had only two occupants between 1852 and 1901 – Mr Timothy Healey, who gave St Mary's Church its gas lighting and was generous in offering the use of his grounds, but seems not to have been accepted because he was "in trade"; and Mr and Mrs J. P. Kitchin, who have already been mentioned in connection with the Welcome Coffee House and the Chalet Mission Hall.

Garrick's Villa was so named after Eva Garrick's death by her solicitor, Thomas Carr, who lived there till his death in 1839. He was followed by Silvanus Phillips, a wealthy London merchant, whose widow remained there for a few years after his death. The next owner was Edward Grove, a very successful restaurant proprietor in London. After Mr Grove's death in 1875 his widow lived in the house until it was bought by the London United Tramway Co.

A history of St Albans by A. F. Kelsall has been published by the Twickenham Local History Society. One occupier, Sir William Wightman, has already been mentioned. The one best known to Hampton was Mr R. G. Graham whose family lived in the house for some 85 years, and who founded the fire brigade. Lord Charles Fitzroy, 2nd son of the 4th Duke of Grafton, and therefore a descendant of Charles II and the Countess of Castlemaine, lived at St Albans for a short time about 1861 before moving to The Elms, the fate of which was to be burnt down by suffragettes in 1913.

In 1892 Charles James Stutfield came to live at Grove House and some 14 years later caused a great deal of speculation when he built what came to be described as a mosque, supposedly because of his conversion to Islam while serving with the British Army in India. The facts were that the "Indian Army Colonel" retired from the Army as an acting Captain and that he never went further afield than

Gibraltar; and he was also a staunch Anglican. There can be no doubt that the so-called mosque was modelled on the Alhambra, which he may well have visited while stationed at Gibraltar.

A well known occupier of one of the Riverdale houses was Mrs French Sheldon, who achieved distinction as one of the first women to explore the African continent. While living at Riverdale she was visited by H M Stanley. She had to leave her house when the owner, Mr F J Kent, sold the block to the Southwark and Vauxhall Water Co., who demolished it to make way for the Riverdale Works.

Sir Henry Knight, a London merchant, lived at a late nineteenth century house called The Elms in the Lower Sunbury Road. Sir Henry became Lord Mayor of London in 1883. One of the many offices he held was that of governor of the Lady Eleanor Holles School while it was still at Cripplegate.

HAMPTON IN 1900

Hamptonians who could remember the middle years of the century doubtless marvelled at the changes which had taken place by the end of it. They would have recalled the disappearance of but a few old houses and the building of very many new ones. Houses old and new mostly had gas laid on and there were plans for an electricity supply. Water was being piped to most houses and wells were becoming a thing of the past. Modern sanitation was replacing the old cesspool. Health was improving; the U.D.C. had a very competent Medical Officer; Hampton had its first District Nurse; and plans were afoot for the building of the Isolation Hospital in Uxbridge Road, completed in 1904.

The greatest changes of all were in the field of communications. The railway already provided a rapidity of travel to and from London which has not been exceeded. As regards local transport, the trams were soon to afford a rapidity and reliability which cannot be attained today. The bicycle was having its heyday and the first motor car had been seen in Hampton, both being encouraged by the asphalting of the roads, which was in full swing by 1900. The telegraph was a commonplace; the telephone was about to be connected; and the postal service was at the peak of its efficiency.

At the turn of the nineteenth century Hampton was probably a more closely knit community than at any other time before or since. The celebration of the Queen's Golden and Diamond Jubilees by all and sundry and the wide appeal of the flower show and the watermen's regatta had helped to foster a community spirit which became more enthusiastic with a growing pride in the achievements of the Fire Brigade, the local athletes, and the Volunteers fighting in the Boer War. Paradoxically Hampton, with its greatly increased population, now wished to be regarded as a village, whereas a hundred years earlier the much smaller community had insisted on being called a "Town".

MAIN SOURCES

Orders of Vestry 1792 – 1846
Churchwardens' Accounts 1766 – 1900
Orders of the Committee relative to the Affairs of the Poor 1803 – 1829
Orders of Select Vestry 1820 – 1836
Court Rolls of the Manor of Hampton Court
Land Tax Assessments 1780 – 1832
Registers of Licensed Victuallers 1800 – 1828
Minutes of Kingston Board of Guardians
Minutes of Trustees of Hampton Free Grammar School 1792 – 1833
Account Book of Private Schools in Hampton
The Surrey Comet 1854 – 1914
History and Topography of Hampton-upon-Thames H. Ripley 1884

Brief History of Hampton School	B. Garside	1957
Ordnance Survey Maps	1804-06,	1864-70 and 1894-96
Enclosure Award Maps	1811-26	
Various Directories	1806 – 1900	

ACKNOWLEDGMENTS

Special thanks are due to the Parochial Church Council of St. Mary Hampton, to the Greater London Record Office (Middlesex Section), the Public Record Office and the Headmaster and Governors of Hampton Grammar School for providing ready access to the records in their charge and to Mrs D. E. Ablewhite for the drawings which form Plates 1 and 3.